D0982874

JOSÉ LÓPEZ RUBIO

IN AUGUST WE PLAY THE PYRENEES

(*Celos del aire*)

Translated by Marion Peter Holt

ESTRENO
University Park, Pennsylvania
1992

ESTRENO Contemporary Spanish Plays 2
General Editor: Martha T. Halsey
                    Department of Spanish, Italian and Portuguese
                    College of the Liberal Arts
                    The Pennsylvania State University
                    University Park PA 16802 USA

Library of Congress Cataloging in Publication Data
López Rubio, José, 1903-
    In August We Play the Pyrenees
    Translation of: Celos del aire
    Contents: In August We Play the Pyrenees
    1. López Rubio, José, 1903-   Translation, English.
I. Holt, Marion Peter. II. Title.
Library of Congress Catalog Card No. 92-72823
ISBN 0-9631212-1-9

Published with Support from

The Program of Cultural Cooperation Between
Spain's Ministry of Culture and the United States Universities
Office of Culture of the Spanish Embassy, Washington DC
The Pennsylvania State University

Cover: Jeffrey Eads

A METAPLAY FOR ALL SEASONS

An elderly couple. with a country home in the mountains and declining income, solve their economic problems by renting out part of the house to a young couple. To maintain their privacy they devise a little farce: each couple will pretend the other does not exist. Only the elderly butler will be able to "see" and "hear" the inhabitants of both worlds. At the play's beginning, the audience is not let in on the joke. The spectators' bewilderment yields to understanding and then) laughter as friends of the young couple enter, unwittingly, onto this stage of theatricalized life.

The fanciful metatheatrical devices of *In August We Play the Pyrenees* are not limited, however, to this one pretense. Cristina, the young wife who chooses the isolated house in the Pyrenees for a summer refuge, is obsessively jealous of her husband Bernard; she is forever inventing imaginary rivals. When their friends come to visit, Enrique, a playwright, plots to cure Cristina by having his own wife Isabel adopt the role of Bernard's lover. But Enrique's play-within-the-play, to which the elderly couple becomes the audience, is, in fact, the truth. When Cristina realizes this, she creates a new script, in which Enrique whispers sweet nothings to her (actually the European capitals with major playhouses), thus arousing Bernard's jealousy and ending the Bernard-Isabel relationship. The visitors leave and the elderly couple breaks their silence to help Enrique and Cristina achieve reconciliation.

On one level, *In August We Play the Pyrenees* is light bourgeois comedy, ideally suited for summer and community theatre. On another level, however, the various plays-with-the-play have a subversive effect, for they mirror the games that the spectators themselves play, reminding us to what extent society functions on hypocrisy and the glossing over of infidelities.

The play requires only one set and seven actors.

In 1986, when López Rubio's *In August We Play the Pyrenees* played in summer stock in Illinois, a local reviewer questioned why it had taken so long for a work of this caliber to cross the Atlantic. The question is indeed a valid one. First staged in 1950, this delightfully inventive comedy is as fresh today as it was then. In 1990-91 it enjoyed a highly-acclaimed revival in Madrid; the original text, *Celos del aire*, was subsequently staged in New York City's Thalia Spanish Theatre. Not limited in its appeal by either time or geography, *In August We Play the Pyrenees* invites discovery by American theatre-goers.

Phyllis Zatlin
Rutgers, The State University

José López Rubio

ABOUT THE PLAYWRIGHT

José López Rubio (b. 1903) is truly the complete man of the theatre. By the age of 27 he had won a major drama competition and had seen his first two plays (written in collaboration with Eduardo Ugarte) professionally staged in Madrid. In 1930 he was contracted by M.G.M. to go to Hollywood to write Spanish versions of their new talking pictures, and in the film capital he became a close associate of Charles Chaplin and other leading figures of Hollywood's "Golden Age." At the end of the Spanish Civil War, he returned to Spain and directed films until resuming his playwriting career in 1949 with *Alberto*. The following year, *Celos del aire* (*In August We Play the Pyrenees*) established him as Spain's leading creator of serious comedy. *La venda en los ojos* (*The Blindfold*), *La otra orilla* (*The Other Shore*), and more than a dozen other comedies and dramas followed.

For almost two decades López Rubio was also a leading translator and adaptor of American stage successes. He provided the first Spanish version of Arthur Miller's *Death of a Salesman*, which exerted a strong influence on a whole generation of young Spanish dramatists, and versions of *The Miracle Worker*, *Two for the Seesaw*, and *Man of La Mancha*, to name a few. He has also translated Molière, Montherlant, Oscar Wilde, and Somerset Maugham into Spanish. In the 1970's he turned to television and wrote two successful and critically acclaimed series, *Al filo de lo imposible* (*At the Edge of the Impossible*) and *Mujeres insólitas* (*Exceptional Women*). The latter, some thirteen dramatizations of the lives of famous women from Cleopatra to Lola Montes, introduced a totally new technique for filmed biography.

In 1983 Spain's senior playwright was elected to the Real Academia Española, thus attaining the highest honor than can be bestowed on a Spanish writer. After an absence of more than a decade, López Rubio returned to the theatre in 1986 with a serious drama entitled *La puerta del ángel* (*The Way of the Angel*). On the opening night of the highly successful revival of *Celos del aire* at Madrid's Centro Cultural de la Villa, in December 1990, the veteran dramatist walked on stage to receive the ovation of a new generation of theatergoers.

José López Rubio *Celos del aire (In August We Play the Pyrenees)* Madrid, 1949.
Photo: Gynes

STAGE SET

The action of the play takes place in a large country house in the Spanish Pyrenees, during the last days of August of a year without war in our own time

CHARACTERS

Doña Aurelia
Don Pedro
Gervasio
Cristina
Bernard
Isabel
Enrique

ACT I

The sitting room of a country house situated in the Pyrenees very near the French border. A mixture of French chateau and northern Spanish manor house, with suggestions of an English country place. Probably constructed in the mid-eighteenth century, it has since been subjected to several remodelings dictated by the taste of its successive inhabitants. The proportions of the room should give some indication of the importance and size of the structure. Upstage, three pairs of glass doors that open on a terrace which serves as an entrance to the house. We can imagine extensive gardens in the background. At least one of the pairs of doors should always be open. At right, two steps and an archway which serves as the entrance from the adjoining rooms and from which the beginnings of a stairway to the upper floor can be seen. At left, a fireplace. Although there is not a lighted fire at any time, the area has, through custom, become the most inviting corner of the room--and for this reason, it is where a great part of the action should be played. DOÑA AURELIA and DON PEDRO will always occupy the two comfortable chairs on either side of the fireplace. Centerstage, a long table with a large crystal lamp with cloth shade. A number of objects on the table, among them an old pistol. Downstage, in front of the table and facing the audience an English-style sofa as long as the table. At one side of the sofa, an easy chair; and in front of it, a small table with ashtray. No old portraits, or tapestries, or suits of armour, or displays of ancient weapons. A grandfather clock. And on the walls, old maps and framed romantic engravings in color. A great globe of the world; and only a few books. Beside one of the fireplace chairs, a sewing table. Much silence, much order, and a suggestion of a severity that derives from good taste.

When the play begins, it's after six in the afternoon. Toward the end of the second scene, the long twilight of summer will begin to fade in an almost imperceptible manner. On different tables there are two tea services--each with two cups which have already been used. One of these services is on the small table near the fireplace where DOÑA AURELIA and DON PEDRO are seated in the two armchairs. Both are more than seventy years old and are dressed in dark clothes with a care for traditional elegance. They are two people with the exquisite upbringing of another century and a gravity of manner that is slightly comical. DOÑA AURELIA, without glasses, is involved with an unnecessary piece of needlework. DON PEDRO is carefully fixing postage stamps in his album, first studying and re-studying them through a large magnifying glass. There are several moments of silence. GERVASIO enters almost unheard from right. He is an old retainer, dressed in a black doublebreasted jacket with wing collar and white bow tie. He is holding several letters and some newspapers still in their wrappers. In a very pronounced and visible manner, he reads the addresses and places the envelopes and papers, one by one, on a silver tray that is on the long table at centerstage. DOÑA AURELIA and DON PEDRO, who have been aware of

GERVASIO's entrance and actions, follow him closely with their eyes. When h has completed his task, he turns towards the left. Then DOÑA AURELIA asks:

AURELIA: Has the postman come, Gervasio?
GERVASIO *(Hesitatingly)*: I'm not sure what I should say to Madam...
AURELIA *(Sharply)*: The truth, Gervasio!
PEDRO *(Gravely)*: Always the truth and nothing but the truth.
GERVASIO *(Unsure)*: It's just that...the truth...as for the postman...
AURELIA *(Impatiently)*: Will you never learn to speak up!
GERVASIO *(Sadly convinced)*: No, Madam. I've never developed the art.
PEDRO *(To D. AURELIA, with gentle reproof)*: Perhaps you have neve developed the art of asking questions. In these difficult times we live ir every question should suggest its own reply. A quick answer that neithe violates nor touches upon the truth.
AURELIA *(With a skeptical smile)*: For example.
PEDRO *(To AURELIA)*: Just listen, *(HE clears his throat; to GERVASIO)* Wa there any mail for us today, Gervasio?
GERVASIO *(Rapidly and with satisfaction)*: No, sir, there was no mail for yo today...
PEDRO *(To AURELIA)*: Do you see how easy it is? *(Delighted with his formula* There was no mail for us, and that settles that.

(GERVASIO bows and is about to exit)

AURELIA *(To GERVASIO)*: Take away the tea service, Gervasio.
GERVASIO *(After looking alternately at the two tea services that are in sight* Which one, Madam?
AURELIA *(Dryly, pointing to the one near her)*: This one. There's no other te service in this room. Is it possible that you see another one?
GERVASIO *(Very certain)*: No. No, Madam. *(GERVASIO picks up the tea servic that DOÑA AURELIA has indicated. Before leaving, he asks)*: Madam...?
AURELIA: Speak up.
GERVASIO *(Timidly)*: Supposing...Just supposing...there were another te service...
AURELIA *(Severely)*: Gervasio!
GERVASIO: I only said "supposing"...
AURELIA *(Impatient)*: Well, "supposing" what?
GERVASIO: Might I--supposing--remove that other tea service to the kitchen?
AURELIA *(Nervously)*: There are things one just doesn't ask!
PEDRO *(To GERVASIO, gently)*: Yes, of course you may remove it.
AURELIA *(Sharply)*: But it's not to go beyond a supposition.
GERVASIO: Oh! No, Madam. *(He takes the other tea service from the table. A he picks up the tray, a napkin falls to the floor)*

AURELIA *(Unable to control herself)*: The napkin, Gervasio!

(GERVASIO looks at the floor and then at DOÑA AURELIA.)

GERVASIO *(Ingenuously)*: What napkin, Madam?

AURELIA *(Regaining control)*: Supposing that...

PEDRO *(Diplomatically)*: Pick up that supposed napkin just as if it were really there.

GERVASIO: Ah! As you wish, sir.

(He picks up the napkin and exits right with the two trays. DOÑA AURELIA sighs as if overwhelmed by the weight of a recent misfortune. DON PEDRO looks at her and shakes his head in a manner indicating an affectionate reprimand.)

AURELIA: It won't work. Don't you realize now that it isn't possible? We're all going to end up crazy...

PEDRO *(Reassuring her)*: Not quite, my dear.

AURELIA *(Protesting)*: You, of course, have your stamp collection. It's easier for you. You have something to distract you. But I'm faced with the reality of every hour.

PEDRO: Still...

AURELIA *(Insisting)*: You've already seen how Gervasio behaves...I don't know if it's pure spitefulness or what...and all the others too. *(Sigh.)* We've tried to go too far.

PEDRO *(Softly)*: It was you who...

AURELIA *(Sadly)*: Yes, I know it was my idea...You don't need to remind me...But...

PEDRO *(Consoling her)*: Come now!

AURELIA: It's more than I can handle...much more...And there are still two months left.

PEDRO: The worst part is already over. Are you going to give up now?

AURELIA *(very dejected)*: For two months more, I don't know. Two months, when you think about it, are nothing. If you don't measure them on the face of a clock. But when you start to think of each hour...It's the hours that frighten me. And the minutes that make up the hours. And the days that never seem to change...Every morning when we wake up it's the same day...*(DON PEDRO takes her hand affectionately; pulling herself together quickly)* Yes, I know it was my idea...But I can't convince myself that we're alone in the house, that we've been alone for two months...

PEDRO *(Smiling)*: Just as we've always been...

AURELIA: More alone than ever. Before, we didn't think about being alone, and now we have to remember it at every moment of the day.

PEDRO *(Trying to cheer her up)*: But within two months...
AURELIA *(Sighing)*: ...we'll be alone, completely alone, just you and I...
PEDRO: ...as we are now.
AURELIA *(With a sigh)*: I'm going to think I'm dreaming when we're back t
being alone as we are now!... *(DON PEDRO pats DOÑA AURELIA's han*
affectionately.) I tell you I'm going to think I'm dreaming...

(At this moment she stops and makes a sign to DON PEDRO. He look
towards the right. Neither says a word; they have heard footsteps. CRISTIN.
enters from right. She is a young woman and is wearing a light colore
summer suit. She has a man's grey jacket in her hand. She does not notice
or pretends not to notice, the presence of DOÑA AURELIA and DOI
PEDRO. She goes to centerstage and, after looking cautiously towards th
right, begins to search for something eagerly in the pockets of the jacket sh
is holding. DOÑA AURELIA and DON PEDRO ignore CRISTINA'
entrance. They remain silent. During the rest of the scene, they pretend nc
to notice the presence of strangers and exchange glances only at certai
points. BERNARD enters from right. He is CRISTINA's husband and a fe
years older than she. He is wearing the trousers and vest that belong wit
the grey jacket she is searching. He is holding a navy blue coat in his hanc
He stops in the doorway when he sees CRISTINA searching through th
pockets of his coat. CRISTINA turns her head and stands there looking c
him and smiling.)

BERNARD *(To CRISTINA)*: Listen, Cristina, wouldn't you be just as happ
rummaging through the pockets of this other suit? I'd like to finish dressing
CRISTINA *(With absolute naturalness)*: Yes. Give it to me.

(BERNARD goes over to CRISTINA and they exchange coats. BERNARI
puts on the one that matches his trousers. CRISTINA leaves the blue coat o
the table and ignores it.)

BERNARD *(Noticing that CRISTINA has not searched the coat)*: Ah! Don't yo
want to continue your little investigation?
CRISTINA: For what? You've probably already inspected it before...
BERNARD: Sure...You were hoping to find what you were looking for in thi
one. Right?
CRISTINA *(Very certain)*: No. I didn't expect to find anything.
BERNARD: Then...
CRISTINA *(Correcting herself with a smile)*: There was still a slight chance
might.
BERNARD *(Smiling in spite of himself)*: What were you looking for? A picture
A lock of hair? A faded flower?...

CRISTINA *(Nodding; simply)*: Or a letter.

BERNARD: Oh! Do you still believe I get love letters?

CRISTINA: Less than I used to.

BERNARD: You're finally convinced?

CRISTINA: I always look through the mail when it comes, and that way I satisfy my doubts.

BERNARD: If you don't find proof, that must mean there isn't any.

CRISTINA: Now let's get it straight. That only means I don't find them. Nothing more. *(BERNARD looks at CRISTINA, controlling himself. Then HE looks at the mail GERVASIO left on the table.)*

BERNARD: Have you gone through today's mail?

CRISTINA: No, I didn't realize it had come... *(BERNARD picks up the letters from the table.)*

BERNARD: Do you want to go through it with me?

CRISTINA *(Pretending indifference)*: All right.

BERNARD *(Reading one of the envelopes)*: From the bank. Anything suspicious about that?

CRISTINA *(Laughing)*: Not at all. *(BERNARD leaves the envelope on the tray. CRISTINA has a sudden idea. Quickly.)* Banks employ women, don't they?

BERNARD: I suppose they do.

CRISTINA *(Almost pondering)*: A female employee has access to the bank stationery...

BERNARD: Certainly. *(HE picks up the envelope again and looks at it menacingly.)* Let's unmask the mysterious woman in the checking department. *(HE. starts to tear open the envelope but CRISTINA stops him with a gesture.)*

CRISTINA: No. Why do that?

BERNARD: Shall I open it or not?

CRISTINA *(After a moment of doubt)*: Go ahead. *(BERNARD opens the envelope. Smiling.)*

BERNARD *(Showing her the contents of the envelope)*: Just a bank statement. No secret messages, no hint of perfume. There *is* an illegible signature--like all important signatures. Satisfied?

CRISTINA: More than satisfied. Did you think I didn't already know it was your bank statement. *(BERNARD gives her a knowing look.)* Yes, of course. Don't look at me that way. Why would I think otherwise? *(BERNARD picks up another envelope and studies it.)*

BERNARD: From Australia...It has a green stamp with a kangaroo. *(DON PEDRO sits up and looks toward BERNARD nervously until DOÑA AURELIA reprimands him with a stern look. HE reaches for his stamp album and begins to search through it anxiously. To CRISTINA.)* From your brother. Do you want to open it?

CRISTINA: I suppose. It will say the same thing he always says. *(BERNARD carefully removes the stamp from the letter.)* What are you doing?
BERNARD *(Raising his voice a bit)*: I'm tearing off the stamp. Didn't I tell you It's green, with a kangaroo. We've never had one like this...

(DON PEDRO has confirmed the absence of the stamp in his album and looks towards BERNARD again with great interest.)

CRISTINA: Are you going to keep it?
BERNARD *(In a loud voice)*: No, I'm going to dispose of it right now.

(HE places it, with great care, on the opposite end of the table. DON PEDRO smiles, looking at him with an expression of gratitude.)

CRISTINA: For a moment I thought you had taken up stamp collecting.
BERNARD: Don't worry. I haven't come to that yet.

(DON PEDRO resents BERNARD's words and turns away properly offended. DOÑA AURELIA smiles with a certain mischievousness. BERNARD returns to the tray of mail and picks up a newspaper.)

BERNARD: The newspaper is beyond suspicion, isn't it?
CRISTINA: I should say! You have to read between the lines.
BERNARD *(Takes the last letter from the tray; showing the letter)*: And this one from my office...Does the stationery convince you?
CRISTINA: The stationery seems authentic. By the way, how many envelopes do you order at a time?
BERNARD *(Offering her the letter)*: Five thousand for routine business. A thousand more for my love letters. Here, open it.
CRISTINA *(With amusing dignity)*: I would never allow myself to open a letter addressed to you.
BERNARD: If I ask you to...
CRISTINA: I'd never read it unless you read it first.
BERNARD: You prefer to read it when you discover it in my coat pocket or in the back of a drawer.
CRISTINA: Yes. It's more respectable.
BERNARD: And what if I dispose of it after I read it, burn it, for example.
CRISTINA: The ashes would be an obvious indication of guilt.
BERNARD: And if I throw the ashes to the wind?
CRISTINA: The smell of the burnt paper would remain--and that's very incriminating.
BERNARD *(A little tired of the game)*: All right. And if I read it in front of you, would you watch me?

CRISTINA: I'd pretend to be doing something else; but, yes, I'd watch you discreetly.
BERNARD: And if I became noticeably upset?
CRISTINA: Certain reason for suspicion.
BERNARD: And if I read it indifferently?
CRISTINA: I'd think:"He's hiding something."
BERNARD *(Crumples the envelope in his hand nervously)*: All this over one letter!
CRISTINA *(Laughing)*: And I'm certain it's from your office.

(BERNARD takes a breath and begins to pace nervously around the room.)

BERNARD: It's not possible! *(HE stops, excited, in front of DON PEDRO and asks)* Can a man live with a woman like this?
DON PEDRO *(Rapidly, without time to reflect)*: To tell the truth, no.

(DOÑA AURELIA gives him a ferocious look. Intimidated, he shrinks into his chair.)

CRISTINA: Who were you talking to?
BERNARD: No one, to myself. *(A brief silence.)*
AURELIA *(To DON PEDRO)*: Did you say something?
PEDRO: No. Nothing...
AURELIA: I could have sworn you did...
PEDRO: No. No.

(Another brief silence. BERNARD, a bit calmer, returns to CRISTINA's side. HE puts his hands on her shoulders.)

BERNARD: Fine. The mail has come. There are no suspicious letters.
CRISTINA: There are letters that don't come by mail.
BERNARD: Then how do they come? They don't fly through the air.
CRISTINA: Oh, but they do Bernard. You're forgetting about air mail.
BERNARD: Come now!...You're thinking about secret messengers, carrier pigeons, bribed servants...
CRISTINA: Mysterious footsteps...prearranged signals.
BERNARD: An envelope without an address...A crumpled piece of paper.
CRISTINA: A message written in lemon juice... *(THEY BOTH laugh.)*
BERNARD: How silly you are!
CRISTINA *(Shrugging her shoulders)*: We'll see...
BERNARD *(After looking towards the garden)*: Do you want to go for a walk this afternoon?
CRISTINA: No, I can't, I still have to search the pockets of your brown suit...

BERNARD: Come here...If what you suspect were true, would I be stupid enough to leave my compromising letters in my pockets with the ends sticking out?

CRISTINA: The least suspicious places are the best for hiding things...

BERNARD: Do you really expect to find a letter?

CRISTINA: If I'm lucky!...

BERNARD: But...what letter?

CRISTINA: Any letter. You tell *me*.

BERNARD *(Worked up)*: I? *(Managing to get control of himself.)* Do you have any reason to think that I have a lover?

CRISTINA: No. No reason.

BERNARD: Aha!

CRISTINA: But I don't have any reason to think that you don't.

BERNARD: Where? How?

CRISTINA: Don't ask me.

BERNARD: Here? You chose this place to spend the summer--a thousand miles from nowhere.

CRISTINA: Oh, you don't have one here.

BERNARD: Well, that's progress. For the moment at least, my lover isn't here.

CRISTINA: Don't get so riled. You act like a child. Let's drop the subject. *(BERNARD looks at her.)* Let's suppose she doesn't even exist.

BERNARD: First you would have to suppose she did exist.

CRISTINA: That's already supposed.

BERNARD: By you.

CRISTINA: Naturally. You're the only one who can't suppose it. For you, fortunately, the question has no grey areas. You must be certain that you have a lover...or that you don't.

BERNARD: I don't.

CRISTINA: I didn't ask you.

BERNARD: But I'm telling you just the same.

CRISTINA: Don't get aroused. When all is said and done, it wouldn't be anything of importance.

BERNARD: No?

CRISTINA: Absolutely nothing.

BERNARD: Then what are you worrying about?

CRISTINA: Because it's easy. Because it's natural. Because it's human. Because it's possible. Because you belong to that man's world out there...

BERNARD: You're jealous, aren't you?

CRISTINA *(Reacting with a smile)*: Haven't you realized by now that I'm just a bit jealous?

BERNARD *(Pretending to be surprised)*: No. Really?

CRISTINA *(Passionately)*: Terribly!

BERNARD *(With irony)*: Poor girl! You must suffer a lot...

CRISTINA *(Smiling)*: Well, sometimes, yes...a lot.

BERNARD (*Deciding to make a joke of it*): If I can be of any help... (*CRISTINA gives a look.*) In killing ghosts, for example. That other woman, whose whereabouts are unknown...whose name is unknown. (*CRISTINA starts to interrupt him.*) Let me go on...That woman, what kind of income does she have?

CRISTINA: How should I know? That's her business...and yours, in any case.

BERNARD: And yours...

CRISTINA: Mine?

BERNARD: If I give her money, where does that money come from?

CRISTINA: How do you expect me to know?

BERNARD: My accounts, our accounts, are an open book.

CRISTINA (*With great dignity*): The last thing I'd ever do would be to inspect your bank account.

BERNARD: You really wouldn't do that?

CRISTINA: Well, I said it would be the last thing I'd do...Anyhow, I don't see why you should have to give her any money.

BERNARD: She gives me money then.

CRISTINA: I doubt that. You don't need money. But maybe she doesn't need it either.

BERNARD: Ah! She loves me for myself, with no ulterior motive.

CRISTINA: Why not? When you and I married we didn't have anything. And didn't I love you without any ulterior motive? Haven't I kept on loving you just for yourself?

BERNARD (*Smiling, flattered*): I believe you do.

CRISTINA: Idiot! Well, it's the same with her...

BERNARD: The same, no. You married me.

CRISTINA: Because you were single. She got into the act late. But maybe she's married too!

BERNARD: Another play?

CRISTINA: The same play, with more characters.

(*CRISTINA remains thoughtful.*)

BERNARD: What are you thinking about?

CRISTINA: He probably loves her as much as I love you!...

BERNARD (*Shouting in exasperation*): Who?

CRISTINA: Her husband.

BERNARD (*Shouting*): What husband?

CRISTINA: Your girlfriend's. Who else?

(*BERNARD, now desperate, crosses and sits on the sofa.*)

BERNARD: Fine!

(CRISTINA goes over and sits on the arm of the sofa close to BERNARD SHE puts her arm around his shoulder tenderly.)

CRISTINA: Let's see. If you had a lover, you wouldn't tell me about it, would you? *(A silence.)* Say something...

BERNARD *(With little feeling)*: Of course not!

CRISTINA: You see? You say no, just as if you didn't have one.

BERNARD *(Protesting, in anger)*: I don't have one!

CRISTINA: You say that, and you always say it in the same tone, with the same frown...whether it's true or a lie. How am I ever going to know it you're deceiving me?

BERNARD: Would you prefer a confession?

CRISTINA *(Terrified)*: No, for God's sake! *(She brings her face close to his looking him in the eyes.)* Don't ever tell me! Do you understand? Even if it's true, even if I see it with my own eyes, you mustn't tell me...

BERNARD *(Joking again)*: Very well. Are you happy that way? Are you happy just not hearing it?

CRISTINA: No. But I need room for doubt. *(BERNARD lets his body slump forward and lowers his head. CRISTINA caresses his hair affectionately.)* I won't search your pockets anymore, if it bothers you...

(BERNARD is silent. DOÑA AURELIA and DON PEDRO have watched the end of the scene intently, without pretense. A brief silence, CRISTINA looks up when she hears some sound from outside.)

CRISTINA: Did you hear something?

BERNARD: What?

CRISTINA: SShhh! *(SHE listens.)* Yes. They've arrived. *(BERNARD looks at her.)* Isabel and ENRIQUE.

(BERNARD stands up. THEY go to the upstage doors.)

BERNARD: Ah, so they have.

(THEY go out on the terrace, looking toward the left.)

CRISTINA *(almost shouting)*: Hello! We're over here!

(CRISTINA and BERNARD exit. We hear the sound of voices from offstage. DON PEDRO gets up cautiously and goes to the table where BERNARD left the green stamp with a kangaroo on it. DOÑA AURELIA follows his movements with her eyes.)

AURELIA: What are you going to do? *(DON PEDRO stops just when he has almost touched the stamp with his hand.)* It doesn't belong to you.

PEDRO: Someone threw it away...Don't you see it? God knows how long it'll stay there! It doesn't belong to anyone. It's mine. It's green, and it'll complete the set. *(While HE is speaking, HE has picked up the stamp and, admiring it, returns to the fireplace. Voices are heard from offstage. To DOÑA AURELIA, uneasy.)* Wouldn't it be better if we left?

AURELIA *(With great dignity)*: Why? We're in our own house. We're alone. We weren't expecting anyone. Do you think that anyone could come?

PEDRO: No, no. But just the same. We *are* so alone! The sunset seems more irreparable when one is inside. Besides, I have the feeling that if we stay here, in a moment or two our aloneness is going to increase.

AURELIA *(Rising)*: Well, if you insist. But it's only another of your obsessions.

PEDRO *(Agreeing)*: Of course, of course. *(He takes DOÑA AURELIA by the arm and leads her toward the upstage doors.)*

AURELIA *(Hesitating)*: Through the hall, if you don't mind. The garden is too lonely at sundown.

PEDRO: Ah! Yes. So it is.

(THEY exit slowly, with dignity, through the archway at right. We hear the sound of voices, and then CRISTINA and BERNARD enter with ISABEL and ENRIQUE. ISABEL and ENRIQUE are a married couple of approximately the same age as BERNARD and CRISTINA. They're dressed for summer, and ISABEL has a scarf over her hair. ENRIQUE is wearing a checked jacket and marroon slacks. HE is carrying a raincoat and cap. They have arrived by car after a trip of four or five hours, with stops for lunch and for admiring the scenery.)

ISABEL *(Entering)*: ...and the road up is beautiful too.

ENRIQUE: We stopped four or five times.

ISABEL: Six.

ENRIQUE: You're right. Seven. We had to stop for oil in Vera.

ISABEL: Gas.

ENRIQUE: Gas and oil.

ISABEL: You didn't mention anything about oil to me...

ENRIQUE: I mentioned it to the man at the station. That seemed more practical than telling you. In any event, you wouldn't have been able to do anything about it.

ISABEL: How do you know? Probably...

CRISTINA *(Laughing)*: Isabel's right. You men never give us a chance to show you... *(To ISABEL.)* Do you like the grounds?

ISABEL: It's all so lovely.

ENRIQUE: Just like France.

ISABEL: Well, we are close.

CRISTINA: Right next to the border.

BERNARD: So close that a part of the estate is on French territory.

ENRIQUE: I hope I won't need a passport to get to the bathroom.

BERNARD: I don't think so. But the water in one of the taps is French.

CRISTINA: The cold water. The hot water is always Spanish.

ENRIQUE (*Looking out from the terrace entrance*): Really, it smells like France...Perfume, good cooking, good grammar...

CRISTINA: On certain days. Then the wind changes and we get the sea air.

BERNARD (*To ENRIQUE*): Tell me. What's it like?

ENRIQUE: What's what like?

BERNARD (*With a touch of nostalgia*): The sea.

ENRIQUE: Well, the way it's always been. Maybe a little older.

BERNARD: I mean San Sebastián, Biarritz...

ENRIQUE (*Catching on*): Oh, where the action is!

CRISTINA: They'll think you were brought here against your will.

BERNARD: Well, not exactly against my will.

CRISTINA: Or kidnapped. (*To ISABEL.*) Don't think it was all my idea--and even if it was, you'll have to admit that it was worth it...

BERNARD (*Without enthusiasm*): Oh, yes.

ENRIQUE: But it is a little out of the way...

ISABEL: And hard to find.

ENRIQUE: We missed the road three times.

ISABEL: Four times, Enrique.

ENRIQUE: Once it was that shepherd's fault, He didn't know right from left.

ISABEL (*To CRISTINA*): Are you two here all alone?

CRISTINA: Completely alone.

ISABEL: Without telling a soul?

ENRIQUE: No one can say you didn't keep your secret well. When we wrote you, we felt almost like spies, and we went out at night with false beards to mail the letter.

ISABEL: And we had to invite ourselves.

CRISTINA: For heaven's sake! Don't talk like that. You know you didn't need an invitation.

ENRIQUE (*Referring to ISABEL*): She was having a fit to see your hiding place. If I hadn't gotten the idea of writing you, I think she would have taken matters into her own hands.

ISABEL: Don't exaggerate. You were the one who had the idea in the first place.

ENRIQUE: Yes, that's true. But who kept insisting that I should have the idea?

ISABEL (*To CRISTINA*): Are our bags upstairs?

CRISTINA: Yes, would you like to freshen up?

ISABEL: Yes, (*To ENRIQUE*) Are you coming?

ENRIQUE: I'll be right up.

CRISTINA: Make yourself at home, I'll take that.

(CRISTINA takes a raincoat that ISABEL left on a chair, and the two go toward the right.)

ENRIQUE *(To ISABEL)*: Don't be too long. They may dine early in this castle.

CRISTINA *(To ISABEL as they exit right)*: Through here. This is the great hall...The bedrooms are upstairs.

ENRIQUE: It really is impressive...And the silence! When I leave the city to work, I always try to find a hotel room with as much noise as possible.

BERNARD *(Sighing)*: What I wouldn't give for a little noise! *(ENRIQUE looks at him with surprise.)* Any kind of noise. Car horns, subways, radios...screeching brakes, and a few loud drunks.

ENRIQUE *(Watching him closely)*: You're that bored?

BERNARD: More than you can imagine.

ENRIQUE: Then why don't you leave?

BERNARD: It's too soon to talk of leaving.

ENRIQUE: Why did you come here in the first place?

BERNARD: It's too late to talk of that.

ENRIQUE *(After studying BERNARD for a moment)*: Well, you've certainly gotten away from it all. Not a house for three kilometers. Not even any people on the highway. Of course, it's not exactly a highway. We couldn't even find it on the road map. *(HE takes a map from the pocket of his raincoat.)*

BERNARD: Not on your map. That's for motorists. *(HE gets up and goes over to an old map hanging on the wall.)* But look here... *(ENRIQUE goes over to the map.)* It's on this eighteenth-century map.

ENRIQUE: So it is! Navarre...France...The Pyrenees...Your directions. But where are we really?

BERNARD: In the eighteenth-century. Don't you see? A modern man is lost in a place from another century, where there're no real connections with the present. A man from our time can hardly breathe here...he becomes restless; and either he adapts to the past or he dies...

ENRIQUE: Have you tried to adapt?

BERNARD: Yes. It's no use.

ENRIQUE *(Both return to the sofa and sit down)*: When are you planning to die?

BERNARD: Go on, laugh. I'd like to see you here.

ENRIQUE: You're looking at me.

BERNARD: I mean in my situation.

ENRIQUE: What *is* your situation?

BERNARD *(Without answering the question)*: You've just come from a place where there are crowds of people. You've brought their sounds with you. The remnants of their conversations are in the creases of your clothes.

(ENRIQUE instinctively brushes off his suit with his hand.) You still hav
the memory of all those human faces.

ENRIQUE *(Philosophically)*: Often I feel more alone in a crowd than in th
middle of a desert.

BERNARD: That's the kind of loneliness I need. Loneliness in the midst of
million people.

ENRIQUE: Who found this place?

BERNARD: Cristina. Who else? Who can isolate me, put me into limbo, bette
than she? She saw an ad in the paper--a house with I don't know how muc
land and forest, an ancient summer retreat of some king of Navarre...Twent
rooms, a carriage house, a chapel...For an unbelievable price.

ENRIQUE: Just for the two of you?

BERNARD: Just for the two of us.

*(At this moment, DOÑA AURELIA and DON PEDRO enter upstage. They'v
been for a walk. ENRIQUE shows his surprise when he sees them come in
He looks at BERNARD. The light has begun to fade. ENRIQUE, uneas
about the apparitions, stands up.)*

BERNARD: Where are you going?

*(With a gesture ENRIQUE indicates the presence of the old couple t
BERNARD. BERNARD looks in the direction ENRIQUE is pointing and the
looks back at him questioningly, as if he hadn't seen a thing.)*

BERNARD: What is it?

*(DOÑA AURELIA and DON PEDRO take their customary chairs. SHE pick
up her sewing; DON PEDRO studies his papers.)*

BERNARD: Did you see something?

ENRIQUE *(Sitting down, worried)*: No.

(He continues to glance cautiously toward the left.)

BERNARD *(To ENRIQUE)*: What's wrong? Have you been working too hard?

ENRIQUE *(Concerned)*: No. *(Pulling himself together.)* What did you say?

BERNARD: I asked if you'd been working these last two months.

ENRIQUE *(Preoccupied)*: Uh-huh...

BERNARD: You aren't paying attention to me.

ENRIQUE: Yes I am.

BERNARD: I asked if you'd written anything new.

ENRIQUE: And what did I answer?

BERNARD: Nothing.

ENRIQUE: What should I answer? I don't know the game.

BERNARD: Whether you've written anything new or not...

ENRIQUE: No! *(Regaining control; in another tone.)* Yes! I've finished a play that I'm quite pleased with. And I've started a comedy about ghosts...

BERNARD: Do you believe in ghosts?

ENRIQUE *(With misgivings)*: Do you?

BERNARD *(With certainty)*: Not I.

ENRIQUE *(Closing his eyes)*: Neither do I. *(After a moment of thought.)* Listen...haven't you noticed anything peculiar about this house?

BERNARD: Peculiar?

ENRIQUE *(Glances left again)*: Something odd like...

(DOÑA AURELIA and DON PEDRO cross the stage slowly and exit right. ENRIQUE, nervous, has stood up again and is watching their departure.)

BERNARD *(Calmly)*: Like what?

ENRIQUE: But...can't you see?

BERNARD: No.

(DOÑA AURELIA and DON PEDRO are now offstage. The deepening shadows during the scene have contributed to the effect their exit has produced on ENRIQUE.)

ENRIQUE: But...did you really not see them?

BERNARD: Yes. They're the owners of the house.

ENRIQUE: Do they come every night?

BERNARD: Every night.

ENRIQUE: When did they die?

BERNARD: Oh, they haven't died yet. *(BERNARD gets up and turns on the lamp on the table.)* That's right. They're the owners of the house. The ones who rented it to us.

ENRIQUE: Are you angry with them?

BERNARD: No. Why?

ENRIQUE: You didn't say hello.

BERNARD: Because I don't see them.

ENRIQUE: Well, if you can't see them at that distance, I'd recommend a seeing-eye dog.

BERNARD: Cristina doesn't see them either.

ENRIQUE: Oh, she doesn't either. Well, then, what's the joke?

BERNARD: There's no joke. It's simply an arrangement. The owners of this estate, people who once had a substantial fortune, now find themselves in financial difficulties. They got the idea of renting out the place during the

summer. Since it's enormous, they decided to rent only part of it. Th
tenants can live completely separate from them. Actually, this sitting roor
and the great hall are the only areas we have in common. And, of course
the gardens. Now do you understand?

ENRIQUE: I think I do. But there's still something peculiar...

BERNARD: For these people, this house and its traditions are an inseparable pa
of their lives. And to have to resort to renting their own home t
strangers...At the same time, we couldn't feel a sense of freedom or intimac
with other people around. Then the old lady hit on the most brillia
solution.

ENRIQUE: Which was...?

BERNARD: That we would mutually ignore one another. That we simpl
wouldn't exist for them. We agreed not to see or hear them, and they woul
close their minds to us. We lead our lives as if we were completely alor
in the house. We are reciprocally invisible. Cristina and I have rented a
empty house. Now do you understand?

ENRIQUE: Yes...

BERNARD: Well, it isn't easy.

ENRIQUE: Although I do write for the theatre, I'm not exactly lacking
imagination. In short, everyone goes about his business without having
say Good Morning or talk about the weather. If your paths cross, you simp
keep on talking as if no one were there...You *do* keep on talking?...

BERNARD: Yes.

ENRIQUE: You don't feel inhibited?

BERNARD: Not in the slightest.

ENRIQUE: And what about them?

BERNARD: It's the same. Both parties have observed the rules faithfully.

ENRIQUE: But what about us?

BERNARD: You'll do the same. You're our guests and you belong to our grou

ENRIQUE: And we can't see them either...and they don't see us. Right?

BERNARD: Exactly.

ENRIQUE: And since this place was so impressive and out of the way--with t
advantage of an invisible landlord--you rented the house for four months

BERNARD: Cristina rented it. It was a *fait accompli*. As soon as she saw that v
could be completely alone...

ENRIQUE: The same old Cristina, eh?

BERNARD: The same--or worse.

ENRIQUE: Is she jealous again?

BERNARD: Not again. She's never stopped being jealous; and with the count
air she's gotten worse.

ENRIQUE: Is that what you meant before when you mentioned your "situation

BERNARD (*Thinking*): I don't know. Probably. (*After a brief silence.*) Don't yo
see? She isolates me, she builds a wall around me...She studies n

expressions, every move I make...At times, I'm afraid to think, because I have the sensation she's reading my thoughts. And we're never apart. When I don't talk, my silence arouses her suspicions. When I sleep, she watches me breathe...

ENRIQUE: And if you snore?

BERNARD *(Nervously)*: I don't snore! I don't even sleep...Who could sleep knowing that someone is watching him dream--expecting to see a name formed by his lips?

ENRIQUE *(Who has been thinking of another matter)*: Does she have a reason for all this?

BERNARD: What did you say?

ENRIQUE: I said: does Cristina have a reason to be jealous...Are you having an affair?

BERNARD: Oh...you know I'm not.

ENRIQUE: I don't know anything.

BERNARD: People always know that.

ENRIQUE: Almost always.

BERNARD: Why would I hide it from you! We've never had any secrets.

ENRIQUE *(Looking at him with suspicion)*: Did I tell you about Margarita?

BERNARD: Which Margarita?

ENRIQUE: It doesn't matter which Margarita...Did I tell you about her or not?

BERNARD: I don't remember.

ENRIQUE *(Helping him)*: Seville...Orange blossoms...Manzanilla in a rustic tavern. A convenient flat tire on a country road.

BERNARD: I don't remember that.

ENRIQUE: Of course not, I never told you. *(With a new doubt.)* And what about the countess? Naples...Vesuvius...fried fish in Santa Lucía. *(He looks hard at BERNARD.)* And the fling I had with Tootsie in California? Ocean Park. A full moon over the Pacific...Hot dogs and sarsaparilla... *(BERNARD's expression infuriates him.)* I didn't tell you anything! I've never told you anything and you've never confided in me...You're a bastard!

BERNARD: Because I've never had anything to tell you.

ENRIQUE: Really? *(He thinks for a moment.)* Then I'm the bastard!

BERNARD: Maybe.

ENRIQUE: No. A man can be with another woman and still not be unfaithful. But there've been nights when my wife thought she had me safe beside her, and I was deceiving her with my thoughts, my desires--which is really what counts. Ah, but women shouldn't be so concerned about us. Perfect infidelity is hard to achieve. It takes too much effort. The wear and tear isn't worth it. And then you start feeling guilty on top of everything else...If what you say is true, your wife ought to put you on an altar.

BERNARD: But you see what she does.

ENRIQUE: Jealousy can kill.

BERNARD: According to my calculations, she has enough energy left for a few more years. But I...I'm at the end of my rope!

(HE becomes pensive and shows his weariness. ENRIQUE is thinking too, leaning back on the sofa and looking at the ceiling. HE starts to laugh. BERNARD looks up in surprise.)

ENRIQUE *(Laughing)*: You could do something about it.
BERNARD: What? What are you laughing about?
ENRIQUE: Do you want to cure your wife? I mean *really* cure her, in a radical way, forever...? Do you want her to stop wondering if you're deceiving her?
BERNARD: What do I have to do?
ENRIQUE: Deceive her.
BERNARD: Do you know what you're saying?
ENRIQUE: Better to face once and for all the danger that one fears rather than fear it forever.
BERNARD: Shakespeare could have written that.
ENRIQUE: He did. I borrowed it from him. Cure her of this sickness, of her jealousy...with the truth. Put the evidence under her nose. She'll either get well or die, *(BERNARD, frightened, is about to say something.)* But she'll be cured. No one has died of jealousy yet.
BERNARD: What about love...
ENRIQUE: Not love either. Do you think Romeo and Juliet loved each other that much? Why, they had to resort to daggers. Don't worry. What is it that's bothering her? Suspicions. Well, as soon as she's certain, she won't have any more reason to be suspicious.
BERNARD: Being certain could be worse than suspecting. And there'd be no turning back.
ENRIQUE: It can all be a game. You can pretend you're deceiving her. We'll just arrange for her to discover you with your lover.
BERNARD: But I don't have one!
ENRIQUE: You'll have one, but she won't really be your lover. She'll only exist so that Cristina can discover her...
BERNARD: She'll discover *her* and kill *me*.
ENRIQUE: Well, that's always possible...but didn't you say you were desperate? And if she doesn't kill you, you can tell her it was all in fun. If she does kill you, Isabel and I will tell her the truth. That should be a great consolation. You've got to begin tomorrow.
BERNARD: And where am I supposed to find a woman!
ENRIQUE: That's the least of your worries. For the time being, a few hints will be sufficient.
BERNARD: But someday that suspicion will have to turn into flesh and blood. And that requires a woman.

ENRIQUE: Then we'll look for one.

BERNARD: Where?

ENRIQUE *(Thinking)*: It is a problem...The only women here are your wife and... *(Suddenly inspired.)* Mine! That's it! Mine!

BERNARD *(Sitting up with a start)*: What?

ENRIQUE *(Delighted with his own brilliance)*: Yes, man. It's perfect. You can deceive Cristina with my wife!...

BERNARD: That's risky business...

ENRIQUE: It's just between us. We've been friends all our lives. And our wives are friends, *(Delighted with himself)* That gives it an even more sinister touch...

BERNARD *(Not very convinced)*: We don't know if Isabel will go along with this.

ENRIQUE: I'll take care of that. She'll try anything. You don't know her. And she'll play her role beautifully. She has an imagination! That's where I get all the ideas for my female characters. When I first met her, she was Teodora in *Majestic*. Do you remember *Majestic*?

BERNARD: Was it a hotel?

ENRIQUE *(Piqued)*: It was one of my plays, imbecile. I married her and then she became Leocadia in *Love on the Instalment Plan. (Angrily.)* That's another of my plays. After two years, she was a different woman--cold, distant, silent--Alexandra in my *Port of Shadows.*

BERNARD: I remember.

ENRIQUE *(Angrily)*: You don't remember.

BERNARD: It takes place in a brothel, doesn't it?

ENRIQUE *(Irritated)*: No! You don't go to the theatre very much, do you? I'm not surprised. Only intelligent people go these days.

BERNARD *(With no desire to debate the point)*: What's she like now?

ENRIQUE *(Not getting the point)*: What do you mean?

BERNARD: What's Isabel like now?

ENRIQUE: Ah! Then I started letting her be the characters from my plays. I only had to give her a sketch of the type, and she would begin to live the character, filling in all the details as only a woman could. When I wrote *Mademoiselle Louise*, she went around speaking French for three months-- and with a Marseilles accent. Last winter I wrote *The Great Lie*--another play of mine you probably won't see...

BERNARD: I promise I will. Go on.

ENRIQUE: I needed a woman who was deceiving her husband--a poor wretch. At night, when I came home, before I started writing, I'd ask her what Maria-- the woman in the play--would have done that day. You have no idea! Secret rendezvous in the most improbable places--Cafes that no one ever goes to, in the most nondescript streets. Small restaurants on the highway outside the city. And jumping into a cab to avoid being seen by the husband. And a magnificent crocodile purse she said she'd bought on sale but was really a gift from her lover. We spent the evenings dying of laughter...Isabel isn't one woman; she's a hundred different women. Sometimes she's so new, so surprising, that I feel like an adulterer just being with her. As soon as I tell her what we have in mind, you'll see, she'll be perfect in the part. She'll even fool you.

(The voices of CRISTINA and ISABEL are heard offstage.)

BERNARD: Careful!

ENRIQUE: Leave it to me. By tomorrow, she and I will have it all planned. *(CRISTINA and ISABEL enter from right. ISABEL has changed her dress. ENRIQUE gets up.)* What? So soon.

CRISTINA: We'll have dinner whenever you're ready.

ISABEL *(To ENRIQUE)*: What a house! You can't imagine, our room is fantastic...

ENRIQUE: If I may...I'll wash up a bit. Is it this way? *(To BERNARD.)* Will you go with me?

BERNARD *(To CRISTINA)* Show him..would you?

CRISTINA: Of course.

ENRIQUE *(To ISABEL)*: Have you seen the ghosts?

ISABEL: What ghosts? *(Catching on.)* Oh, yes!

CRISTINA: I've told her everything.

ENRIQUE: Then you know that we can't see them either.

ISABEL: Yes. Go on, love. Don't keep us waiting.

ENRIQUE *(To CRISTINA)*: Don't bother...Just tell me where it is.

CRISTINA *(Who has picked up BERNARD's blue coat)*: I have to go anyhow, to take this...

(THEY exit left. They are talking together as they exit. ISABEL has moved over to the garden door. BERNARD remains standing near the sofa with his back to the audience.)

ISABEL *(In a cold and indifferent voice)*: Is it cold here at night?

BERNARD: Rather cold.

ISABEL *(Returning to centerstage)*: Do you plan to stay here much longer? *(Before BERNARD can answer, SHE goes to his side and speaks in a lower voice, with passion and reproach.)* Why haven't you written me?

BERNARD *(Uneasy)*: I couldn't, I told you it was impossible.

ISABEL: I couldn't bear being apart from you, without hearing. You don't know what I had to invent to come to see you. And you don't deserve to be loved the way I love you!

(SHE throws her arms around him. BERNARD, nervous and afraid of being caught, tries to pull away and to convince ISABEL of her rashness.)

BERNARD: Don't be a fool! Don't you understand? They may come back any minute.

ISABEL: I don't understand anything!

(SHE kisses him passionately. BERNARD ends up taking her in his arms.)

A VERY QUICK CURTAIN

ACT II

*It's three-thirty in the afternoon on the following day. DOÑA AURELIA and
DON PEDRO are onstage in their customary chairs. ISABEL is seated on the sofa
reading a book. ENRIQUE is stretched out on the floor in front of her. He is
surrounded with sheets of paper and is writing. A half-a-glass of whiskey is
nearby. On the table, a tray with a bottle, ice bucket, glasses, and siphon. ISABEL
is wearing light-colored summer attire; ENRIQUE, sweater and slacks. DOÑA
AURELIA is embroidering and DON PEDRO is reading the morning paper from
San Sebastián. No one is talking. ENRIQUE writes one or two lines; then he re-
reads what he has written. Without taking his eyes off the sheet, he picks up his
glass and takes a sip. He puts the glass down, thinks a moment, and scratches his
head with a pencil. He laughs to himself and starts to write again. He tosses the
finished page aside and shifts position. With a clean sheet in front of him, he
thinks and scratches his head again. He looks off into space and then speaks to
ISABEL without turning in her direction.*

ENRIQUE: How would Jenny tell the millionaire that she can't accept his love?

ISABEL *(Without looking up from her book)*: Who is Jenny?

ENRIQUE: Jenny's a frivolous girl.

ISABEL: And she doesn't accept the millionaire's love?

ENRIQUE: No. She can't. She loves another man.

ISABEL: One who has more money?

ENRIQUE: No. A lot less.

ISABEL: Then she's not a frivolous girl.

ENRIQUE: She's frivolous all right, but inexperienced.

ISABEL: If she were experienced, she wouldn't be frivolous.

ENRIQUE: Why?

ISABEL: Because experience is what puts an end to frivolity.

ENRIQUE *(Pointing to the book that ISABEL is reading)*: Is that what your book
    says?

ISABEL: No.

ENRIQUE: Who says so then?

ISABEL: I do.

ENRIQUE *(Closing his eyes)*: Say it again.

ISABEL *(Tired of the subject)*: I don't remember what I said.

ENRIQUE: Experience is what puts an end to frivolity. What a false truth! *(He
    sits up in a kneeling position and leans closer to ISABEL as if to convince
    her of something very important.)* What happens is that frivolous people
    have frivolous experiences. Don't you see?--Faithful to their frivolity until
    death. On the other hand, levelheaded people are born sensible...

ISABEL: Nobody is born sensible.

ENRIQUE: Uf! Some people are deadly serious when they're born! Haven't yo
ever noticed how some babies look at you...with such deep seriousness tha
they seem to be judging you? *(HE looks hard at ISABEL.)* You've bee
talking nonsense all day. *(Happy with his discovery)* Like Jenny! Of course
That's the way Jenny would talk! Thank you very much!

ISABEL *(Going back to her reading)*: You're welcome.

*(ENRIQUE stretches out on the floor again to write. HE takes a sip of hi
drink.)*

ENRIQUE: They'd order oysters first. Jenny doesn't like oysters.

ISABEL: You see, she isn't so stupid after all.

ENRIQUE: But the millionaire loves them. If millionaires didn't like oysters, onl
shipwrecked people would eat them. Right?

ISABEL *(Who hasn't been listening, but just to say something)*: Yes.

ENRIQUE: What did I just say?

ISABEL: I don't know.

ENRIQUE: Well, you agreed with me.

ISABEL: It's easier than disagreeing with you.

ENRIQUE *(Delighted)*: Of course! *(HE writes it down.)* Jenny should agree wit
everything because it's the easiest thing to do. If she said no, she wouldn
be frivolous any longer. *(ISABEL looks up from her book withou
understanding what ENRIQUE is talking about. HE writes.)* A dozen oyster
for the millionaire. No. Two dozen.

ISABEL: Is he a multimillionaire?

ENRIQUE: For the moment at least.

ISABEL: Are they in a restaurant?

ENRIQUE: Of course they are! That's a stupid question. Where else would the
order oysters? In a fish market? *(With an air of mystery)* They're in a
expensive restaurant...and in a private room.

ISABEL: Already?

ENRIQUE: This millionaire doesn't waste time. That's how he got to be
millionaire. He knows the value of time! But he knows nothing of the jo
of wasting it. Two dozen oysters.

ISABEL *(As SHE continues to read)*: You should only eat oysters in months tha
have an "r".

ENRIQUE: Don't worry. It's January.

ISABEL: How do you know?

ENRIQUE: Because Jenny is dreaming about a fur coat.

ISABEL: Women dream about fur coats all year round.

ENRIQUE: But now it's urgent. *(HE writes.)* Jenny also orders oysters.

ISABEL: But she doesn't like them!

ENRIQUE: So she won't give herself away. Besides, she thinks she might find a pearl.

ISABEL: Does she?

ENRIQUE *(Seriously)*: No, this isn't a play about miracles. It's a drawing-room comedy, where everything happens just as it does in real life. Oysters don't have pearls; but millionaires do. He has a string of pearls in his coat pocket.

ISABEL: For Jenny?

ENRIQUE: He always carries a spare for emergencies. In case he has to get a girl into bed or leave the country in a hurry.

ISABEL: Ah, then, the pearls are real?

ENRIQUE: Of course they're real!

ISABEL: And will Jenny get them?

ENRIQUE: We still don't know. It's up to her. No millionaire in the world is going to hand over a string of pearls for nothing. That's strictly for the middle-class. We won't know until the second act.

ISABEL: What happens in the second act?

ENRIQUE: I don't know. I haven't gotten that far yet.

ISABEL: Do you suppose she'll cause his ruin?

ENRIQUE: I doubt it. He has too much money. At least he can hold out until the third act. And then we'll see. It depends on the price of explosives. He has more explosives than anyone in the world.

ISABEL: I hope he keeps them in a safe place.

ENRIQUE *(Delighted)*: Of course. That's what Jenny will ask him. She thinks it could be dangerous. Every time the millionaire lights up a cigar, Jenny starts to tremble.

(HE begins to write animatedly. ISABEL has been back in her book for some time. DOÑA AURELIA and DON PEDRO have listened to the previous dialogue with growing astonishment.)

AURELIA: Do they really put such things on the stage?

PEDRO: I'm afraid they do.

AURELIA: And they don't burn down the theatres?

PEDRO: I don't know. Sometimes, yes, a theatre burns and all the costumes and scenery with it.

AURELIA: Why would people pay to see such nonsense?

PEDRO: *Chacun a son gout*, my dear.

(ISABEL and ENRIQUE · have heard the conversation between DOÑA AURELIA and DON PEDRO. ISABEL smiles, giving ENRIQUE a malicious look. He turns around in pique. GERVASIO enters from right with the tea service for the older couple. He places it near them on a small table.

ENRIQUE watches GERVASIO's movements. He changes to a sittin
position on the floor.)

ENRIQUE *(To ISABEL)*: The servant...is he visible?
ISABEL: I think he is at certain hours.
ENRIQUE: Do you suppose he's visible at tea time?
ISABEL: I don't know.
ENRIQUE: I'll put it to a test. *(GERVASIO has placed the tray on the tabl*
ENRIQUE tries to get his attention), Hssss, you. *(GERVASIO turns his hea*
in ENRIQUE's direction and looks straight through him, but ENRIQU
doesn't give up.) Hssss!

(DOÑA AURELIA and DON PEDRO are watching closely.)

AURELIA: What is it, Gervasio?
GERVASIO: Nothing, madam. I thought I heard something.
PEDRO: So did I. But there's no one around.
AURELIA: It's a bumblebee that flew in from the garden. He's been buzzing h
head off all afternoon.
GERVASIO: It's an insect all right.

(ISABEL smiles. ENRIQUE doesn't see the humor. HE has an idea and take
a bill from his pocket.)

ENRIQUE *(Showing the money to GERVASIO)*: Hssss!
GERVASIO *(Ready to be of service the moment HE sees the bill)*: I'm on m
way, sir.
AURELIA *(Sharply)*: And where are you planning to go, Gervasio? Didn't I te
you it's only a bumblebee?
GERVASIO: Indeed, madam. I'm only going to see what it wants. *(HE bow*
politely and goes to centerstage. To ENRIQUE) Did you wish somethin
sir? *(ENRIQUE takes his empty glass and hands it to ISABEL, who, in tur*
passes it to GERVASIO. HE takes the glass and pours a shot from tl
whiskey bottle on the table.) How's that sir?
ENRIQUE: A little more. I'm going to be alone a few days. *(GERVASIO fills tl*
glass to the point ENRIQUE indicates. Then HE finishes filling the gla
with soda.) Excellent. By the way, do you know if there are mice in th
house?
GERVASIO: Why do you ask, sir?
ENRIQUE: Because I've been hearing some strange noises. Especially from th
direction.

(HE points toward DOÑA AURELIA and DON PEDRO. GERVASIO glances over.)

GERVASIO: Well, I don't know.

ENRIQUE: Perhaps they're termites.

GERVASIO: Termites? I couldn't say. Ice, sir?

ENRIQUE: Yes, *(GERVASIO puts ice in ENRIQUE's glass. HE hands it to ISABEL who passes it to ENRIQUE. Meanwhile, ENRIQUE has left the bill on the arm of the sofa. Taking the glass.)* Thank you very much. *(Seeing that GERVASIO hasn't moved.)* What are you waiting for?

GERVASIO: I'd like to know, in case I find a bill on the sofa, if it belongs to anyone.

ENRIQUE: No. It isn't mine. You can find it.

GERVASIO *(Reaching for the bill.)*: What a stroke of luck! A bill. *(HE picks it up and looks at it with disenchantment.)* I thought it was a ten.

ENRIQUE *(Searching his pockets)*: It's just that...

GERVASIO: It's all the same, sir.

ENRIQUE: I'll lose another one just like it in my room.

GERVASIO: In what location?

ENRIQUE: On that chair at the right, when you enter.

GERVASIO: A very conspicuous spot. The maid might find it first. It would be better if you lost it inside an envelope with my name on it.

ENRIQUE: Well, I won't forget to lose it. What's your name?

GERVASIO: Gervasio Martínez, at your service. But Gervasio is sufficient.

ENRIQUE: Fine, Gervasio.

GERVASIO: If you need any other extraordinary service...

ENRIQUE: Yes, I already know the fee.

GERVASIO: You must realize, it's a very risky business...If you wish, I could make a special price for the entire season.

ENRIQUE: If you need anything, ask him now before the price goes up.

ISABEL *(To GERVASIO)*: No. Nothing, thank you.

(GERVASIO bows and turns to DOÑA AURELIA and DON PEDRO, who have been drinking their tea with an air of righteous indignation. THEY act as if they haven't seen or heard GERVASIO.)

GERVASIO: Anything more?

AURELIA *(To DON PEDRO)*: Do you recall that servant we used to have? I think his name was Gervasio...

PEDRO: Ah, yes! What ever happened to him?

AURELIA: He disappeared. I don't know if he took anything with him. He wasn't a man you could trust.

PEDRO: He'd sell himself for a counterfeit bill.

AURELIA: He may have died.
PEDRO: I doubt it. Not his kind...He probably ended up in jail...
AURELIA: Well, if he hasn't, he will.

(GERVASIO gives them an indignant look and crosses right. When H. passes near ENRIQUE, HE stops a moment.)

GERVASIO: You were right, sir. There *are* termites.
ENRIQUE: Really?
GERVASIO: Yes. Two of them. GERVASIO exits right. ENRIQUE watches hir go, smiling to himself. ISABEL has gone back to her reading. ENRIQUE happy, hums a tune and looks over what he has written. A line occurs t him, he smiles, and writes hurriedly.
AURELIA *(To DON PEDRO)*: Shall we go outside?
PEDRO: If you wish.
AURELIA: The sun's beginning to go down. *(ENRIQUE laughs out loud whil he writes.)* There's nothing that irritates me more than an insect in a roon
PEDRO: In summer, with all the doors open, almost anything can come inside.

(DOÑA AURELIA stands and DON PEDRO imitates her.)

AURELIA: Thank God for winter! They all die off in the winter, don't they?
PEDRO: At least they go away.
AURELIA: But don't they die too?
PEDRO: Some do. Others, I've read, sleep all winter.
AURELIA: Then that's why they're so stupid in the summer.

(THEY exit. ISABEL has not been listening to this dialogue. Laughin ENRIQUE watches them leave. HE imitates the buzzing of an insect.)

ENRIQUE: Buzzzz!

(BERNARD appears from right. HE stands watching.)

BERNARD: Hello. *(ISABEL looks up and bothered by the sight of BERNARI goes back to her reading. Crossing to the sofa)* You seem to be spending very entertaining afternoon.
ENRIQUE *(Curtly)*: If you say so. We had to occupy ourselves somehow whil you were taking a three-hour siesta.
BERNARD *(Laughing)*: Surely you aren't offended.
ENRIQUE: I was.
BERNARD *(To ISABEL)*: You too?
ISABEL *(Without taking her eyes from the book)*: No.

ENRIQUE: She's only mildly offended. But I'm genuinely pissed. You simply abandoned us after coffee.

BERNARD: I announced that it was the custom here in the country to take a siesta after lunch, and it didn't seem like a bad idea to you.

ENRIQUE: Not bad and not good, but I didn't imagine you'd really given in to country habits.

BERNARD: Since you slept till noon...

ENRIQUE: Naturally. I was born and bred to the city and I never give up any of my prerogatives...whether I'm in the country or on a desert island. I have the ways of a civilized person built into me. I don't see why I should forget any of the basic principles just because there are a few more trees around...or why it's necessary to wake up because a rooster crows at dawn.

BERNARD: So, you did hear him! He'll wake you up every morning just as he does me.

ENRIQUE: No. He won't wake me up again. Or you either. I threw a bottle at him from the window.

BERNARD: Did you hit him?

ENRIQUE: I believe so. At least I hit something with feathers. Look, you should stop being so morbidly interested in nature and start tending to your affairs.

BERNARD: My affairs...

ENRIQUE: Making love to Isabel. *(To ISABEL)* Right?

ISABEL *(Indifferent)*: Of course.

ENRIQUE *(Exasperated)*: You're getting nowhere this way. You should have some consideration for poor Cristina. How is she going to suspect you if she has no motive?

BERNARD: She's always found a way before.

ENRIQUE: But she doesn't suspect Isabel yet. Don't you feel ashamed of yourself?

ISABEL: Enrique!

ENRIQUE: Well, it's true!...He acts as if flirting with you for a few days is an unpleasant prospect. *(To BERNARD)* I warn you. A lot of men have fallen for her. She gets bouquets of yellow roses from a mysterious admirer. When we got married, there was an engineer who threatened to kill himself. *(To ISABEL.)* What *was* his name?

ISABEL: I don't remember.

ENRIQUE *(To BERNARD)*: Yes, man. A tall fellow with glasses who played a lot of golf. His name was...Well, it docsn't matter.

BERNARD: I'm only waiting for instructions. You said you'd plan it all.

ENRIQUE: And don't forget that Isabel and I are doing it just for you. Because we're such good friends and feel an obligation to repay the hospitality you've shown us here...simple as it is. With the amount of imagination I'm using for you I could write a new play. We'll start with a secret meeting some place...

BERNARD: Where?

ENRIQUE: Not too far away. Any place with a romantic setting. For example, canoe on the lake...

BERNARD: What lake?

ENRIQUE (*Indignant*): Ah! You don't have a lake? Then I don't suppose yo have a canoe either. How do you expect me to work without a set an props?

BERNARD (*Suggesting timidly*): Would the rose garden do?

ENRIQUE (*Totally rejecting the idea*): Not enough intimacy.

BERNARD (*After a moment of thought*): The garage...

ENRIQUE: You're too old for that. Don't you have a place that's presentable?

BERNARD (*Timidly*): There's a river...It's not very wide...

ENRIQUE: It'll have to do. The Mississippi won't be necessary. I suppose it ha a bridge at least. A rustic bridge...

BERNARD: It's made of concrete.

ENRIQUE: Concrete! Concrete! What crimes have been committed in your name Well, go wherever you like. The important thing is not to be here whe Cristina arrives. I'll paint the picture in my own way...

ISABEL: You're not suggesting we stay out there until the moon comes up...

ENRIQUE: Give me, at least, until sunset. A sunset, skillfully managed, can b extremely effective.

BERNARD (*To ISABEL with a resigned air*): Shall we go?...

(*ISABEL gets up without enthusiasm.*)

ENRIQUE: Talk about anything you wish, except politics, because she'll see th on your face and it would be counterproductive. (*To ISABEL.*) You can mu up your hair a bit...keeping in mind that you're a married woman. (*T BERNARD*) On the way back, you take Isabel's hand when you're a hundre yards from the house. Or if there're trees, at twenty yards.

BERNARD: Very well.

ISABEL: Can we walk down to the village?

ENRIQUE: Yes--but only if you don't buy anything. Packages would destroy th effect.

BERNARD (*Pointing to his own cheek*): A smudge of lipstick?

ENRIQUE: Too amateurish, that's the first evidence you'd get rid of. Really, wh do you think women carry tissue in their purses? I'm beginning to believ you've never had an affair.

BERNARD: I told you I hadn't.

ENRIQUE (*Pushing him along*): I'll see you later. You'll be amazed how we I've prepared the terrain. I'm going to make it look so suspicious that I'll b jealous of you myself.

BERNARD (*Alarmed*): Watch yourself!

ENRIQUE: Jealous in the best sense of the word. See you later.

(HE exits right. ISABEL and BERNARD exchange glances until HE is offstage and far enough away not to overhear them. BERNARD is uneasy.)

BERNARD *(In a low voice)*: Are you sure he doesn't suspect anything?
ISABEL: Isn't it obvious?
BERNARD: It's a bit too obvious.

(ISABEL moves close to BERNARD and puts her finger on his lips.)

ISABEL: Don't worry. He has too much imagination to notice anything right under his nose. He never reads a book the way other people do. He only looks at the pages and fills in the rest for himself, without bothering with the author's words. When we're talking, he answers questions I haven't asked yet.
BERNARD: Because he already knows what you're going to say...
ISABEL: Because he prefers to invent what I'm going to say. He never listens to anyone because he's always listening to himself. At concerts he substitutes the music in his mind for what the musicians are really playing. At the theatre, he sees an entirely different play from the one on the stage.
BERNARD: But he has two eyes...
ISABEL: He always has a mirror in front of his eyes, where he watches himself...day and night.
BERNARD: And when you make love?
ISABEL: Don't you understand? I'm only the reflection of his own passion. When he makes love to me, he's really making love to himself. That's why we've never had any children.
BERNARD: But he does have you with him. And his arms, and his hands, and his lips...touch you.
ISABEL: Are you jealous?
BERNARD: Of him? Of course I am!
ISABEL: He's the one who should be jealous.
BERNARD: I'm jealous of him because he isn't jealous. He doesn't know about it when I'm with you, but I always know when you're with him.
ISABEL: Even when you know that I'm betraying him with my thoughts by thinking of you?
BERNARD: It has nothing to do with thoughts...when he's breathing the very air you've breathed.
ISABEL *(Smiling)*: Don't be jealous of the air. We sleep with the windows open. You have nothing to fear. Enrique turned out to be a different man from the one I married. To win a woman, a man plays a role...and the role begins to bore him after he's got what he wanted. Even after our wedding I didn't

know him well. You only know a person well when you discover that he' another person. And to that other person I owe no love or fidelity...I mad no promises to his faults, to his obsessions, to his egotism. You see, the ma I married doesn't exist...

BERNARD: And then you noticed me.

ISABEL: I beg your pardon. I noticed that you had noticed me. Until then I ha my mind made up to go along with the farce, to keep on taking cards in hi game of life. I was reconciled to hearing the words of love I'd inspire spoken by actors in his plays. Even while he was speaking them to me, h was thinking how they'd sound in the theatre. He memorized them so tha he could sell them later...He never loved me simply for myself. He stole m words to give them to other women. It was like seeing someone else wearin my jewels. Every love scene, in every play he wrote...he'd rehearsed wit me...

BERNARD: That's why you got even by telling him about our meetings as if yo were making it up...

ISABEL: Perhaps. Did he tell you?

BERNARD: Yes, Isabel. And it was wrong. That was our secret. You've give bits of it away. And that's the worst thing you can do with a secret.

ISABEL: I had to compensate in some way for the pain of knowing that he wa still faithful to me...in his way.

BERNARD: Oh, not all that faithful. Not at all. Seville, Naples, California...

ISABEL: Ah! You know about that? When I found out that he had deceived me my conscience didn't bother me so much...

(BERNARD is about to say something but HE hears footsteps on the terrace DOÑA AURELIA and DON PEDRO appear upstage and go to thei customary places.)

ISABEL *(To BERNARD, in a different tone)*: Well, let's go, so that your wife ca have her suspicions.

(THEY exit upstage. DOÑA AURELIA watches them leave. There's a brie silence. ENRIQUE appears at right. HE goes to the terrace doors. HE see ISABEL and BERNARD go off. CRISTINA enters right. When HE hears he footsteps, ENRIQUE turns around with a broad smile.)

CRISTINA: What are you laughing about?

ENRIQUE: Nothing. I laugh because it's healthy. One should have a good laug every few hours, for no reason at all.

CRISTINA: Where's Isabel?

ENRIQUE: She went out.

CRISTINA: Oh...

ENRIQUE: ...with Bernard.

CRISTINA: Where were they going?

ENRIQUE: I don't know.

CRISTINA: Why didn't you go with them?

ENRIQUE: Well, you see...Bernard said I'd get tired--it's a long walk...Isabel insisted on finishing the restaurant scene this afternoon. She's delighted with my new play! To tell the truth...I realized that they didn't want me to go with them.

CRISTINA: Why didn't they ask me?

ENRIQUE: I suggested that...but Isabel said you were busy with something or other. And Bernard said you didn't like long walks.

CRISTINA: They've probably gone to the caves...

ENRIQUE: What caves?

CRISTINA: Some caves with strange stalactites, not too far from the village.

ENRIQUE *(bothered)*: Why didn't Bernard tell me there were caves with strange stalactites...

CRISTINA: He probably thought you wouldn't be interested.

ENRIQUE: He knows very well they would interest me. The problem is everyone wants to take the initiative around here, *(CRISTINA looks at him with puzzlement.)* They must have gone to the caves. You'll see. *(With a new thought.)* Are they very big?

CRISTINA: Yes. And dark.

ENRIQUE: Could they get lost if they wandered around?

CRISTINA *(Rejecting the idea)*: I don't think they'd try to explore alone.

ENRIQUE: But could they get lost?

CRISTINA: I doubt it.

ENRIQUE: So do I. But if someone could get lost, they could also say that they got lost...

CRISTINA: When?

ENRIQUE: When they get back, if they return late...

CRISTINA *(Surprised)*: Why should they return late?

ENRIQUE: Oh, I don't know...

CRISTINA *(Without seeing the point)*: It's not that far...

ENRIQUE: And, furthermore, as a pretext it would be very crude.

CRISTINA: Why would they need a pretext?

ENRIQUE: Why does anyone need a pretext? To avoid telling the truth.

CRISTINA *(Gradually becoming uneasy from this moment)*: What truth?

ENRIQUE: How do you expect me to know? It's because I don't know what truth that I'm beginning to think of all possibilities.

CRISTINA *(Tense)*: What are you hinting at...?

ENRIQUE *(Denying any importance to what he's been saying)*: Anyhow, it's possible they won't return late.

CRISTINA: I don't understand.

ENRIQUE: I wouldn't want to upset you unnecessarily, but...
CRISTINA: What?
ENRIQUE: There *is* something.
CRISTINA: What kind of "something"?
ENRIQUE: Something they want to hide from me--and, apparently, they don't want you to know either...
CRISTINA *(Anxiously)*: What reason do you have to think...
ENRIQUE: If not, why so much mystery? *(CRISTINA looks at him fixedly without daring to ask.)* Look, I wouldn't suspect Bernard of anything. He wouldn't be capable. But you don't know Isabel. With her anything's possible.
CRISTINA *(Controlling her anxiety)*: Anything? Just what is "anything"?
ENRIQUE: Well, anything is anything. For example: Tonight we could find our beds shortsheeted and we'd have to sleep in the fetal position. There might be firecrackers in the wardrobes. Or she could dress up in a sheet and pretend to be a ghost...or, as the *pièce de resistance* put a goat in the bathroom. Anything, I tell you. Isabel can't conceive of being in the country without having everybody a nervous wreck all night. It's a family illness. She inherited it from a grandfather who was notorious. She knows how I disapprove of all her pranks. But she can't help herself.
CRISTINA *(Laughing with relief)*: And that's all?
ENRIQUE: Isn't that enough? What else could she be up to? Why else were they talking in whispers when I came in? And stopped talking when they saw me? Tell me, for what other reason did they go off together? Why wouldn't they want us to go with them? It's obvious something's brewing. Don't you agree?
CRISTINA *(Beginning to worry again)*: Yes.
ENRIQUE: We should be prepared, just in case. I'm going to lock my room right now. I don't want my mattress levitated or a bucket of water falling on my head when I open the door. That sort of thing went out with the First World War, but Isabel continues to find some kind of perverse pleasure in it. I advise you to be on guard. All that secretiveness and whispering...Tiptoeing all over the place together...There's more than enough reason to be on guard. I'm going to take my own precautions.

(HE exits right. DOÑA AURELIA and DON PEDRO have followed the scene with almost as much concern and suspicion as CRISTINA. CRISTINA remains centerstage, not knowing what to think. A doubt has been born in her mind, and it has nothing to do with what ENRIQUE has been talking about. SHE can't understand how ENRIQUE can be so myopic. SHE's nervous. In her movements and expressions, we can see the following sequence of thoughts as SHE stands looking at the door through which ENRIQUE has exited: "Are they playing a joke on me?" SHE looks up gayly and goes to the table and rearranges some flowers in a vase and feels

somewhat relieved. "Surely it's just as he says: a prank." *SHE smiles, less convinced.* "Yes. A funny prank, a goat in the bathroom." *SHE is rapidly losing faith in this idea, but SHE tries to keep other thoughts at a distance with a movement of her head.* "It can't be," *SHE smiles, ashamed of even thinking it.* "How can I think such a thing of Bernard?" *SHE walks around the table and sits on the sofa, calmer. SHE picks up the book ISABEL has left behind; SHE begins to read, but after a few lines SHE looks up again, with growing suspicions.* "But if they talk together in secret and have gone off together..." *SHE stands and goes upstage. SHE looks toward the garden. SHE starts thinking again.* "Can it be true?" *SHE wants to get rid of her suspicions but can't.* "No. No. It's not true." *SHE looks around in distress.* "My God, what if it were true?" *SHE looks toward the left where DOÑA AURELIA and DON PEDRO have been observing her during the entire scene. SHE's ashamed that THEY may have been thinking the same as SHE.* "They're watching me." *SHE suddenly turns away. DOÑA AURELIA and DON PEDRO have hidden their interest as much as they can.* "Can they know something I don't?" *SHE looks back at them, distraught.* "Is it true? Do you believe it's true?" *Now THEY look at one another openly. There is a terrible tension in the silence. CRISTINA is ready to break down the wall that separates them, in her need to find help. DON PEDRO, looking at CRISTINA, stands up instinctively. HE is about to say something--HE's not sure what. Perhaps HE's going to tell her what HE knows. DOÑA AURELIA looks down at the floor, fearing the explosion SHE believes inevitable. Any word is going to extend a bridge. Then ENRIQUE appears at right. HE quickly grasps the situation. HE smiles at DOÑA AURELIA and DON PEDRO. HE goes over to CRISTINA and, pointing to the wall where CRISTINA is looking, says:)*

ENRIQUE: Yes, its's crooked. I'd already noticed.

(HE goes toward DOÑA AURELIA and DON PEDRO. HE passes between them as if they weren't there and goes to a painting on the wall which is indeed hanging crooked. DON PEDRO sits down and resumes his pretense. DOÑA AURELIA rummages eagerly in her sewing basket. ENRIQUE straightens the painting, looks at it, and turns toward CRISTINA to consult with her.)

ENRIQUE *(Pointing to the painting)*: Is it better now?
CRISTINA *(Who has reacted quickly)*: Yes. Yes.

(ENRIQUE returns to centerstage, after passing between AURELIA and PEDRO again.)

ENRIQUE *(To CRISTINA)*: Heaven knows how many years--or centuries--tha painting has been hanging crooked. In these abandoned old houses, when the owners disappear, everything goes to ruin. *(He sits on the sofa.)* They're taking their time, aren't they?

CRISTINA *(Pretending)*: No...

ENRIQUE: They've probably gone to the village.

CRISTINA: Why don't you go and surprise them?

ENRIQUE: Surprise them?

CRISTINA: Well, find them...

ENRIQUE *(Making himself comfortable on the sofa)*: They'll be back soon, i they're faithful to us.

CRISTINA *(Trying to go along with the jest)*: And if they aren't?

ENRIQUE *(Laughing)*: They'll still be back. Don't worry. Husbands always come back.

CRISTINA: And wives?

ENRIQUE: Almost always. *(Stands up.)* If they return, I'm upstairs. If they don' return, let me know when dinner's served... *(With a mocking tone)* Bu they'll be back. Let's not get our hopes up.

(He exits right. CRISTINA is worried again. DOÑA AURELIA and DON PEDRO watch her. CRISTINA, her mind made up, goes to the upstage door and exits into the garden. DOÑA AURELIA and DON PEDRO follow he with their eyes and then exchange glances. DOÑA AURELIA fixes her eye on DON PEDRO with a reproach from the past. HE looks down.)

PEDRO *(Finding an excuse)*: I...I did come back.

AURELIA: After two years...

PEDRO *(With a poor excuse)*: Transportation wasn't so dependable in thos days...But I did come back.

AURELIA: After I'd given up hope...

PEDRO: And yet...

AURELIA: Yes. I forgave you on the spot.

PEDRO: We could never really be separated.

AURELIA: True. But you gave it a good try.

(There is a moment of silence. The afternoon light has begun to dim ISABEL and BERNARD enter upstage. BERNARD is worried and in a ba mood. ISABEL follows without taking her eyes off him. BERNARD takes ou his cigarette case, takes a cigarette and lights it nervously.)

ISABEL *(Moving closer to BERNARD)*: You aren't certain...

BERNARD: Certain, no. But I think so...

(HE is pensive. ISABEL, casting off all concern goes over and sits beside him on the sofa.)

ISABEL: So, what's the problem? We were playing our roles...in a comedy. Right?

BERNARD *(Not very convinced)*: Yes.

ISABEL: It was my husband's idea. He even cast us in the parts.

BERNARD: Yes, but...

ISABEL: And you may have only imagined it...Who would have been walking in that part of the garden?

BERNARD *(Serious)*: How should I know?

ISABEL *(With a suspicion, looking in the direction of DOÑA AURELIA and DON PEDRO)*: Did you hear one person or two?

BERNARD: I'm not sure what I heard...It sounded like soft footsteps...

ISABEL: Well, whoever it was can do one of two things: Keep quiet about it-- which doesn't help us, because we'd be obliged to repeat the love scene in the garden--or go tell Cristina, which is what we wanted...

(ISABEL has dedicated these sentences to DOÑA AURELIA and DON PEDRO. BERNARD doesn't reply. HE's still worried. ENRIQUE appears. At first HE doesn't notice ISABEL and BERNARD. HE goes to the upstage doors and looks toward the garden. HE turns around and realizes that ISABEL and BERNARD are seated on the sofa in silence.)

ENRIQUE *(Displeased to see them)*: You're here? That's just fine! While I'm busy putting you into the proper landscape, to add a bit of decoration to your guilty passion, you're here inside acting as bored as a married couple. You haven't even taken the elementary precaution of holding hands which is the only thing that can justify a long silence between lovers...And poor Cristina out there looking for you like a raving lunatic...

BERNARD *(Standing up)*: Cristina? Where?

ENRIQUE: I don't know. She went out a while ago.

(ISABEL and BERNARD look at each other.)

BERNARD *(Uneasy)*: Where was she going?

ENRIQUE: Around...to the garden...maybe even to the village.

BERNARD *(Going toward the doors)*: I'm going to see...

ENRIQUE: Yes, yes. Go after her. Show her how much you've missed her, play up to her. And we'll never finish this. Look, at least exaggerate your concern. In the excessive and extemporaneous tenderness of a husband there is always a hint of guilt... *(BERNARD, without hearing him out, exits upstage. To ISABEL, referring to BERNARD)* What's wrong with him?

ISABEL: I don't know.

ENRIQUE: Isn't he acting a little strange? He must be in love, *(ISABEL looks a* *him.)* Yes, that's it. In love with his wife. Poor fellow! He's fed up with Cristina's jealousy but he can't live without her. It's got his adrenalin up. The jealousy of a woman we love renews a man's confidence in himself. You should be jealous sometime...

ISABEL: Of whom?

ENRIQUE: Of me, of course!

ISABEL: You and who else?

ENRIQUE: Oh, whomever you wish. An actress, for example. I spend a lot of time backstage, and everybody knows about actresses...because they spend their lives under a spotlight. Other women can have their adventures in the shadows. This winter you must be jealous of an actress.

ISABEL: Any special one?

ENRIQUE: Do you want me to give you all the details in advance? A star, of course! You wouldn't expect me to get involved with one of those young things who hop into bed just to get a role? I'll leave them to playwrights of a certain age. Do you promise?

ISABEL *(Indifferently)*: Very well.

ENRIQUE: With you jealous I'll probably be as happy as that wretch who's not only in love with his wife but with her jealousy as well. If Cristina wants to hold on to him, she shouldn't lose that singular attraction... *(ISABEL can't listen to any more of this. SHE's nervous and on edge. SHE stands up.)* Where are you going?

ISABEL: I don't know. Nowhere in particular.

ENRIQUE: I'd go with you...it's my favorite destination, but I have to stay here to see what comes next--so I'll know whether to keep on stirring up Cristina's jealousy or put an end to the game and let them live happily ever after in their own sweet martyrdom. *(ISABEL starts toward the door at right.)* At least you were probably seen together.

ISABEL *(About to explode)*: What do I know about it! Leave me alone now, I have a terrible headache.

ENRIQUE: I believe you. You'd never come up with such a trite excuse.

(HE likes the line and takes his notebook to write it down. ISABEL, furious, exits right. After HE has the line jotted down, ENRIQUE gets up and goes to the upstage doors, where HE stands looking out, trying not to be seen from the outside.)

AURELIA *(Sighing)*: My God, what a world! What a world this is!

PEDRO: What's wrong with the world?

AURELIA: I'll never understand why it was created this way.

PEDRO: Would you have done a better job?

AURELIA: Most certainly. Not in six days, of course, I don't see--God forgive me--what the hurry was about in the first place.

(BERNARD's voice is heard from the garden. DOÑA AURELIA and DON PEDRO end their conversation and wait in silence.)

BERNARD'S VOICE *(From the garden)*: Cristina!...Cristina!... *(ENRIQUE listens with the greatest interest, looking toward the garden.)* Cristina!...

(ENRIQUE quickly conceals himself, remaining at one side of the doors. DOÑA AURELIA and DON PEDRO are baffled by his actions. At the same moment, CRISTINA enters hurriedly, as if escaping from something. SHE is upset and shaking. SHE goes to the sofa, trying to regain control and to conceal her emotions. ENRIQUE has gone out one door while CRISTINA entered through another, and now HE reappears. HE stands in the doorway watching CRISTINA. SHE hasn't noticed his presence, although she is aware of the other characters. SHE is fighting a terrible inner battle and ends up collapsing on the sofa in tears. DOÑA AURELIA and DON PEDRO look at her sympathetically. ENRIQUE smiles as if he'd finished the second act of one of his plays to his complete satisfaction. HE turns to CRISTINA.)

ENRIQUE: Ah! Bernard was calling you in the garden a moment ago. *(When CRISTINA hears ENRIQUE's voice, SHE sits up quickly. SHE dries her eyes and tries to pretend as much as possible. ENRIQUE, now at CRISTINA's side.)* Did you hear him?

CRISTINA: No.

ENRIQUE: That's strange.

CRISTINA: I was inside the house.

ENRIQUE: What's wrong with you?

CRISTINA *(Trying to hide her feelings)*: With me?

ENRIQUE: You look as if you've been crying.

CRISTINA: How ridiculous! Why would I be crying?

ENRIQUE: Only you could know that. Crying is a woman's privilege. Men are forced to ration their tears and hold them for special occasions. A pity, because tears can be such fun! I've never believed that crying consoles. It's really a great way to prevent boredom.

(A brief silence, CRISTINA has been thinking while ENRIQUE chatters on.)

CRISTINA *(After a moment of hesitation)*: Listen to me, Enrique.

ENRIQUE: I'll try. But I promise nothing. It's one of those things I don't do very well. Lack of practice, I suppose. Is it something important you want to tell me?

CRISTINA: Not in the slightest...It's really silly.

ENRIQUE: That's a relief.

CRISTINA: Has your wife ever been jealous of you?

ENRIQUE: Well, to tell the truth, it never occurred to me to ask. Maybe yo should ask her.

CRISTINA: You've never given her a reason to be jealous?

ENRIQUE: Oh, yes. Frequently. But only to keep up appearances. I never wen beyond appearances.

CRISTINA: And you...have you ever been jealous of her?

ENRIQUE: Why should I be?

CRISTINA: You've never had that fear--without any basis, of course--that Isabe might be deceiving you?...

ENRIQUE: Occasionally, yes, I've thought about it--as you think of things tha happen to other people but you're certain will never happen to you. The wa we think of death...

(HE is standing near the long table, and HE has picked up, in a jokin, manner, the old pistol lying there.)

CRISTINA: And have you thought about what you would do if...

ENRIQUE: Yes.

CRISTINA *(Unable to conceal her anxiety)*: What? *(For an answer, ENRIQUE- with a smile-- shows her the pistol that HE has in his hand.)* You'd kill her

ENRIQUE: Her? No, *(Making a joke of it)* She knows where all my things are and it would be a nuisance to have to try to find everything after the tria was over.

CRISTINA *(Almost not daring to ask)*: Then...

ENRIQUE *(Suddenly serious and with growing intensity)*: Undoubtedly, I'd kil the man. At the slightest suspicion. *(HE waves the pistol.)* Without eve taking time to hate him. Before the blood rushed to my head and blinde me--they say it happens--because that would take away half the pleasure o killing him. In cold blood. Catching him off guard so that he wouldn't hav time to think of her in his final moments...All I'd need would be th slightest hint. I wouldn't bother to check whether it was true or not.

CRISTINA *(Frightened by ENRIQUE's vehemence)*: And what if he turned ou to be innocent?

ENRIQUE: Even better for him. That would surely appeal to me. If you have t choose between dying innocent or dying guilty... *(HE looks at the frightene CRISTINA.)* Forgive me, I've frightened you. It's your fault. Nobody shoul induce a husband to start thinking about these things. *(HE hesitates an gives CRISTINA a hard look.)* Why did you ask me if Isabel...

CRISTINA *(Quickly)*: No reason. Don't start imagining things.

ENRIQUE: Do you know something?

CRISTINA: Don't be silly. What would I know?

ENRIQUE *(Impatiently)*: Where is Isabel?

CRISTINA *(Worried)*: Upstairs, in her room, probably...but for God's sake calm down...

ENRIQUE *(With a sudden suspicion)*: And Bernard?

CRISTINA *(Forcefully)*: In the garden. Didn't you just hear him. He's alone. Looking for me... *(ENRIQUE starts toward the upstage door with pistol in hand. CRISTINA, crying out)* Enrique! No!

(In the doorway ENRIQUE turns around toward CRISTINA, who is terrified and trembling. HE starts to laugh. CRISTINA looks at him without understanding. HE returns to centerstage, laughing.)

ENRIQUE: You can't deny that we have the ideal conditions for a first-rate melodrama...Your cry was perfect. *(HE leaves the pistol on the table)* Just like a curtain scene. And they still say that the theatre is expensive! *(CRISTINA doesn't understand his words or his change in attitude.)* So this is an example of your famous jealousy, eh? Suffering over him, afraid he'll be unfaithful...Ah, but if he is, don't let anything happen to him. If there must be a tragedy, spare him...wretch that he is. Your jealousy isn't real, Cristina. It's too tainted with love.

(ENRIQUE has sat down on the sofa and is now talking calmly. CRISTINA is amazed.)

CRISTINA: But...what you said...

ENRIQUE: Forget it. An invention to measure your true feelings. Your sad pathetic jealousy. Selfish girl, you thought I'd take the trouble to kill my wife so that your husband could crawl home and beg forgiveness--and be forgiven, didn't you? Don't look at me that way. Everything that's happened here, since yesterday, has been planned.

CRISTINA *(Still in doubt)*: Everything?

ENRIQUE: The idea was mine...and part of the dialogue. They supplied the action.

CRISTINA: Ah! *(After thinking a moment.)* And what about Bernard?

ENRIQUE: Don't worry. I had to convince him, because he was born to be a faithful husband. It was necessary to put your jealousy to a test even though that involved a certain amount of risk. But not too much as I now know.

CRISTINA *(Thinking)*: And he was capable of...

ENRIQUE: You've already seen...

CRISTINA *(Almost to herself)*: Yes, I did see...

ENRIQUE: And now we have to tell them that the game is over and they don't have to play their roles any longer.

CRISTINA: Wait, you said my jealousy was selfish. It's true. But can you
understand what went with it--an almost maternal instinct to defend and
protect him from all danger? Can you understand the torment of wanting to
hate and not being able to? No need to answer. Your game wouldn't be fair
with a single loser--with the others in league against the loser and knowing
all the tricks, you owe me a chance to play a part, and I'm going to have it.
ENRIQUE: How?
CRISTINA: The same way...only this time you and I will be the players.
ENRIQUE: That's a terrible idea. What about poor Isabel?
CRISTINA: It never occurred to you to say "poor Cristina."
ENRIQUE: It's different. Your jealousy already existed. We'd have to create
jealousy in Isabel. It's a much more serious matter. And, furthermore, Isabel
would never forgive me. Women can make an art of reproach. It wouldn't
work.
CRISTINA: Then what you're really thinking is "poor Enrique."
ENRIQUE: Well, I do have to think of myself--since I'm convinced that no one
worries about me as well as I do myself.
CRISTINA: Would you be afraid to make love to me?
ENRIQUE: It's not that I'd be afraid. But you don't know my wife...
CRISTINA: You wouldn't allow me to fall in love with you either?
ENRIQUE: Ah, that's a sign of good taste I've never been able to deny to a
woman...as long as there're no strings attached...
CRISTINA: As long as it's only letting yourself be loved.
ENRIQUE: No problem.
CRISTINA: Your vanity will automatically take care of the rest. I'll praise your
talent, your work, your brilliance...
ENRIQUE: Sincerely?
CRISTINA: What difference does it make? Writers like praise the way women
adore compliments--even when they know they aren't sincere.
BERNARD'S VOICE (From the garden): Cristina!
CRISTINA: There he is. Are you ready?
ENRIQUE (Alarmed): Right now? Without rehearsing?
CRISTINA: Don't worry. For tomorrow we can prepare some special effects. Just
leave everything to me, I'll set the tone, (CRISTINA places herself in a
kneeling position on the sofa close to ENRIQUE, with an eager look almost
of adoration.) Talk to me!
ENRIQUE: About what?
CRISTINA: About anything you wish, but softly. The rivers of the world...the
multiplication tables...Do you know the capitals of Europe?
ENRIQUE: Those that have theatres...
CRISTINA: Tell me their names.
ENRIQUE: Do I start in the north?
CRISTINA: Anywhere you wish.

ENRIQUE: When do I stop?

CRISTINA: When you've convinced me you're so irresistible that I have no choice but to fall in your arms.

BERNARD'S VOICE *(Coming closer)*: Cristina!

CRISTINA: Begin.

ENRIQUE *(Not too sure of himself, mechanically)*: Stockholm, Oslo, the Hague...

CRISTINA: With more mystery, dear...Be more seductive.

ENRIQUE *(In a lower tone)*: Copenhagen...How's that?

CRISTINA: For a start, not bad.

(BERNARD. appears in the doorway and registers surprise when he sees CRISTINA on the sofa beside ENRIQUE. ENRIQUE is now speaking in a low, confidential voice, so that his words can hardly be understood.)

ENRIQUE: Helsinki, Athens, Lisbon, Sofia...

(CRISTINA breaks into laughter as if she'd just heard the cleverest thing in the world.)

BERNARD *(From the door)*: Cristina!

CRISTINA *(As if distracted from a very interesting conversation)*: What? Oh, it's you...

BERNARD: Yes. Didn't you hear me calling you?

CRISTINA: No. Have you been calling me?

BERNARD: For half an hour, in the garden...

CRISTINA *(Hardly listening to him)*: Oh... *(To ENRIQUE, with keen interest)* And then...

ENRIQUE *(Beginning to enjoy the game)*: Just imagine...Warsaw, Paris, Moscow...Tirana...

CRISTINA *(With surprise)*: No!

ENRIQUE: Yes, yes, yes. Budapest and Prague.

CRISTINA *(Laughing)*: You're scandalous!

BERNARD *(Impatient)*: Have you been here all the time?

CRISTINA: Eh?...What did you say?

BERNARD: I asked if you'd been here all the time.

CRISTINA *(With all her attention on ENRIQUE)*: Yes, Quite a while...

BERNARD: And you didn't hear me calling you?

CRISTINA: I don't think so... *(To ENRIQUE.)* And then what?

ENRIQUE: I, you can imagine...Bucharest.

BERNARD: You must have heard me...

CRISTINA: Well, I may have heard you. I'm not deaf. *(To ENRIQUE)* Impossible!

ENRIQUE: Yes, it's true...Monte Carlo, Belgrade.

BERNARD *(Very impatient)*: Cristina!

(But CRISTINA is no longer listening to him. BERNARD, perplexed and bothered, doesn't know what to do. ISABEL appears at right.)

ISABEL: Enrique!

(HE doesn't respond. HE is talking rapidly in a low voice.)

ENRIQUE: Brussels, Madrid, Luxembourg...and Bern.
ISABEL *(After giving BERNARD a look of amazement)*: Enrique!
ENRIQUE *(Absentmindedly, without turning his head)*: What dearest?
ISABEL: Have you seen the cigarettes and lighter?
ENRIQUE *(Absentmindedly)*: No, love. *(To CRISTINA, with intense interest)* And at that moment...Vienna.

(While HE is talking, HE takes from his pocket a cigarette case, extracts a cigarette and lights it with a lighter that HE finds in another pocket. CRISTINA is laughing loudly. BERNARD and ISABEL can only exchange looks.)

CRISTINA: No! That can't be true.
ENRIQUE: Yes. Ask Isabel. She'd never let me tell a lie.
ISABEL: Oh, but I would! As many as you wish.
CRISTINA: Of course I believe you. Go on!
ENRIQUE *(Excitedly, in a low voice)*: Did I say Stockholm, Bucharest...and Budapest...

(CRISTINA laughs in great amusement. ISABEL just looks irritated. BERNARD goes over to her and offers a cigarette. HE strikes a match and extends it to her. THEY can't keep their eyes off CRISTINA and ENRIQUE.)

ENRIQUE: London, Dublin... *(Triumphant)* And Timbuctu!

(CRISTINA is dying with laughter.)

CURTAIN

ACT III

Late morning the following day. ENRIQUE is kneeling on the sofa and using the table as a desk. HE writes a word on a sheet, stops, thinks, scratches his head, makes a wad of the sheet of paper and leaves it on the table beside other similar wads of paper. HE repeats this operation. During this game, DOÑA AURELIA appears alone at right. SHE is carrying a sewing bag. SHE goes over to her sewing table, opens it, and then takes out the piece SHE has been working on and puts it in her bag. Paying ENRIQUE the least attention possible, SHE goes out again at right. ENRIQUE continues to use up pieces of paper after writing a word or two on them. In a moment, GERVASIO enters from right.

GERVASIO: Sir...

ENRIQUE: Eh?...

GERVASIO: If you will permit me, sir, I'd like to speak with you a moment.

ENRIQUE: What's the charge?

GERVASIO: Completely gratis, sir.

ENRIQUE: That's a relief, Gervasio. Because your fees have gone sky high since you joined our team.

GERVASIO: It's the time of year, sir. In summer, in high season, you know how it is. But you won't have further cause for complaint, sir...

ENRIQUE: Why?

GERVASIO: Because I've gone back over to the enemy.

ENRIQUE: How much did they pay you?

GERVASIO: Nothing, sir. It was a romantic gesture on my part.

ENRIQUE: At your age, Gervasio?

GERVASIO: I meant a disinterested gesture.

ENRIQUE: Well, you've done the right thing. One usually gets his reward for disinterested acts.

GERVASIO: The master has sent me on a secret mission--taking advantage of madam's absence. He's in bed...sick. How could I refuse him after all these years in his service? Just imagine, even before he was married. I stayed on when we married madam. And then, when we started cheating on madam...It was even more difficult for me after we made up with her. The usual: Did I do this or know that? Regardless of what I did or didn't do or knew or didn't know, he went off on his own to Rio de Janeiro with a ballet dancer!

ENRIQUE: Yes. In those situations the woman usually forgives the guilty party, but she's implacable with his accomplices.

GERVASIO: However much they hate the crime, they still love the criminal. And now, you see, he has called me to his bedside.

ENRIQUE: To make his last confession?

GERVASIO: No. He did that nine years ago. Since then there's been nothing to confess.

ENRIQUE: Then...

GERVASIO: He asked me--coughing his head off--to come speak with you in a very confidential manner. No one must know about it...especially madam. He even asked me to request your word of honor on this. But I couldn't be that presumptuous.

ENRIQUE: You'd be wasting your time. I never give my word of honor until I know what benefits are in it for me if I go back on it.

GERVASIO: I don't think I understood you well. That course would be a bit immoral, wouldn't it?

ENRIQUE: It depends on your point of view.

GERVASIO: You're probably right. At your age, it's worth the trouble to be cynical. At mine, it no longer has the slightest merit.

ENRIQUE: And what part of your master has suddenly broken down?

GERVASIO: None yet. But last night, with the damp air, he caught a terrible cold. He stayed here longer than customary, with all the doors open, waiting for something to happen...which, according to him was going to happen. And what happened was that today he's in no shape for anything to happen.

ENRIQUE: Poor man! And what can I do about it?

GERVASIO: Well, with the greatest reluctance, he suggests that you arrange things so that whatever is going to happen, happens upstairs in his room. He says it's very spacious and has a balcony door for entrances and exits, so that with a little imagination you could adapt things nicely...

ENRIQUE: What nonsense! With him stretched out in bed?

GERVASIO: He says he would be willing to meet you half way in order to come to an agreement. He would get out of bed, put on his robe, and sit quietly in a chair without bothering anyone.

ENRIQUE: He's suggesting that we shut ourselves up in his bedroom to resolve our personal affairs?

GERVASIO: No. He recognizes that it's a bit unusual; but he says he hasn't slept a wink all night, thinking of what could happen without his seeing it. Because hearing about it wouldn't be the same, *(There is a brief silence. ENRIQUE smiles as thinks it over.)* What shall I tell him?

ENRIQUE: That I'm very sorry...that I'm not the only person involved. There are several of us, and no matter how big his bedroom is...

GERVASIO: Oh, it's big enough. Don't worry about the space.

ENRIQUE: Don't you understand, man? It would seem like an adaptation for television. And, besides, if it turns out he has the flu, it could be dangerous for the performers.

GERVASIO: Of course. But I really don't think it's as serious as the flu. He coughs a lot, to be sure, but I think they're minor germs...

ENRIQUE: As long as one person's coughing, it's hard to hear the dialogue. You know what happens in the theatre. Someone always has a hacking fit at the most crucial moment, and we never find out who inherited the estate.

GERVASIO: These days the servants are the heirs, sir. The theatre keeps up with the times and redistributes the wealth.

(ENRIQUE smiles. GERVASIO is still waiting for his decision.)

ENRIQUE: Tell him it's impossible.

GERVASIO *(Sadly)*: He's going to be terribly upset.

ENRIQUE: The most I can do is see that he gets a copy of the script as soon as we know what's going to happen.

GERVASIO: He'll be most grateful. And so will I...now that we've made up. *(CRISTINA enters from right. SHE is carrying a bag with sewing materials on her arm.)* Would you like a glass of sherry, sir? *(Noting ENRIQUE's hesitation)* It's on the house...

ENRIQUE: No, Gervasio. Thank you all the same.

(GERVASIO bows and exits right. CRISTINA crosses and sits on the sofa.)

CRISTINA: They haven't returned?

ENRIQUE: No. And letting them wander off to play their roles without an audience strikes me as bordering on mental cruelty. To have to pretend to be in love and suspect us at the same time...

CRISTINA: Up to this point we haven't given them much reason to suspect us...

ENRIQUE: Ah! Do you think what we did last night was unimportant? I used up the capitals of Europe and had to jump to North Africa, which I don't know very well...

CRISTINA: Have you written the letter?

ENRIQUE: I haven't been able to finish it. I'm caught between two fires! I've finished the draft of one for Isabel, so she can copy it on her flamboyant stationery and plant it where you can discover it in your husband's pocket.

CRISTINA: Yes? And what does it say?

ENRIQUE: The usual. You'll read it. And now I'm having a hell of a time trying to compose your letter to me.

CRISTINA: I thought we'd agreed that you would write to me.

ENRIQUE: We did, but I've thought better about it. Since it's a matter between you and your husband, it's only natural that you should face the consequences. If I limit myself to being admired, I'm not compromised. But a love letter from me, written to another woman, in Isabel's hands...I don't want to think about that!

CRISTINA: Where's the draft?

ENRIQUE: I've only started it. Didn't I tell you? It's my second love letter from an unfaithful wife in one morning. The one for Isabel was easy, because she's my wife and I know what she'd say. Yours is another matter.

CRISTINA: All love letters are basically the same...

ENRIQUE: They're the same only at the end, when they ask for money...I don't know your style...and Bernard has to believe it's authentic. Do you see my problem?

CRISTINA: Well, you aren't writing literature for posterity.

ENRIQUE *(With his usual self-esteem)*: I...

(HE's about to add: "...am an author, and don't ever forget it.")

CRISTINA: A few pointed lines are enough. "I'll wait for you in such and such a place." Or even better, "in the usual place." It's not too specific and much more compromising.

(DOÑA AURELIA and DON PEDRO appear at right. DON PEDRO is supporting himself on his wife's arm, and HE is noticeably out of sorts. HE's wearing dark trousers and a wool dressing gown with silk collar; a silk muffler around his neck. HE can be wearing bedroom slippers--provided they're expensive. HE should not appear unkempt or too informal. On the contrary, it's obvious that HE has taken great care with his appearance, in spite of his illness, and looks almost elegant. GERVASIO follows them with a lap robe over his arm. We hear DON PEDRO coughing offstage before he is actually seen. HE enters in a real fit of coughing.)

AURELIA: Watch out for the step! *(DON PEDRO responds illhumoredly with something like: "I already know there's a step. Do you think I'm a fool?" Because of the cough his words don't project clearly. He steps down with difficulty.)* It was lunacy for you to get out of bed today...much less come downstairs. *(DON PEDRO coughs; and halfway to his chair has to support himself on the table.)* It won't be good for you.

PEDRO *(Irritated)*: I know that. Some people insist on having their own way-- even if it kills me. Well, I'll die, but seated in the front row.

(With some effort they've reached their seats. CRISTINA does not understand why DON PEDRO is so indignant. ENRIQUE smiles without looking their way. When DON PEDRO is seated, GERVASIO wraps the lap robe around his legs and exits right.)

AURELIA: Come now, just relax. If you get excited, the coughing will start. And when the coughing starts, you'll get more excited. And you'll...

PEDRO: A lot anyone around here cares whether I cough or not! It's obvious, my health counts for nothing in this house!

AURELIA (*Patiently*): I don't know what you're talking about, my dear, you aren't making sense...

PEDRO: My room is almost as big as this one, isn't it?

AURELIA: Yes, but what does that have to do with it?

PEDRO: And just walking through it, I don't see how anyone's going to damage his reputation...

AURELIA: You've lost me completely. I don't see how anyone's reputation could possibly be connected with your bedroom.

PEDRO: The same things can happen in my room that happen any other place.

AURELIA (*Trying to soothe him*): Of course, dear. Anything you want to happen. But let's avoid extravaganzas with animals...that poses unnecessary risks...

(*DON PEDRO, piqued, doesn't answer and lets his cough take over. ENRIQUE smiles. CRISTINA can't figure out what this is all about and looks inquiringly at ENRIQUE. DON PEDRO picks up a newspaper and makes a stab at reading.*)

CRISTINA: Well, where's the copy of my letter?

ENRIQUE (*Showing her the pile of paper on the table*): There, in all that paper. A word or two on each wad, (*HE smoothes out two of all the sheets and compares them.*) If you were writing to me tenderly, how would you begin? "My dearest" or "Dear Imbecile"?

CRISTINA: I'm not sure what I'd call *you*. But for my husband, I'd say: "My dearest."

ENRIQUE: Yes, anything to hide the truth...

CRISTINA: How did you come to specialize in cynicism?

ENRIQUE: Matrimony improved my natural talents.

(*ENRIQUE has unwadded more paper. HE shows the sheets to CRISTINA. When SHE is about to examine them, a sound is heard offstage. SHE goes to the upstage doors and returns quickly.*)

CRISTINA: They're coming.

ENRIQUE: Well, I'm getting out and taking the evidence with me.

CRISTINA: Why bother? There's only one word on each sheet.

ENRIQUE: But what words! My love, my treasure, my life, my wild flower...and all in my handwriting. Don't you understand, Isabel's bright enough to know that after a certain period of time a husband doesn't write that way to his wife--unless he's been away from her for a few months in the wilds of Siberia.

CRISTINA: I'll meet you in the garden in ten minutes to make a brilliant entrance.

ENRIQUE: With no exaggeration, please. Because we wouldn't be so stupid as not to try to hide our feelings a bit; and they aren't so stupid that they wouldn't catch on. It isn't necessary to overdo the note of passion. You can see how discreetly they've handled their own roles.

CRISTINA (*Almost to herself*): That's true (*SHE remains pensive while ENRIQUE exits right with his hands full of paper. CRISTINA is starting upstage when ISABEL and BERNARD appear. There is a pink or violet-colored envelope sticking out very conspicuously from one of the pockets of BERNARD's jacket. CRISTINA stops when SHE sees them. With a hint of disappointment,* Oh, it's you...

ISABEL: Yes.

BERNARD: Who did you think it was?

CRISTINA: No one in particular.

(*SHE goes back and sits in an armchair.*)

BERNARD: So much interest in no one in particular?

CRISTINA (*Pretending surprise*): Interest? Who? Me?

(*With nothing else to do, SHE explores her sewing bag. ISABEL and BERNARD exchange glances. ISABEL makes a sign to BERNARD about the letter in his pocket. BERNARD understands and jerks a button off his jacket.*)

BERNARD: Cristina, would you sew on this button for me?

CRISTINA: Of course. Give it to me.

(*HE goes over with button in hand.*)

BERNARD: There's no hurry.

CRISTINA: *You* may not be in a hurry.

BERNARD: But you are?

CRISTINA: No, but I'll probably...

BERNARD: You'll probably *what*?

CRISTINA: Oh, nothing. (*Impatiently*) Give me the button! (*BERNARD positions himself beside CRISTINA so that the letter in his pocket can be seen. CRISTINA prepares her needle and thread and BERNARD hands her the button.*) It's been ripped off.

(ISABEL has sat down on the opposite end of the sofa. SHE picks up her book from the table and pretends to read--without missing a single detail of the scene.)

BERNARD: How can you tell that?

CRISTINA: It's like fruit. You can tell when it's been plucked off the tree before it's ripe. And, besides, when you came in, your jacket had all its buttons.

BERNARD: They've begun to fall off...Had you noticed that?...

CRISTINA: It's a wife's business to notice if her husband's in one piece. You're going to lose that.

(SHE pushes the envelope back into BERNARD's pocket. SHE prepares to sew on the button.)

BERNARD: Wait. I'll take it off.

CRISTINA: That's not necessary.

BERNARD: I insist. It'll be easier for you.

CRISTINA: There's no reason to do a striptease.

BERNARD: Oh, Isabel won't be shocked.

ISABEL: Don't mind me...

BERNARD *(Taking off his coat)*: You see? Nobody's offended.

CRISTINA *(Referring to DOÑA AURELIA and DON PEDRO)*: We never know when we're being watched.

BERNARD *(Looking at the ceiling)*: True. But I'm getting used to that.

(CRISTINA has taken BERNARD's jacket and placed it in her lap. SHE begins to sew on the button. BERNARD has taken care to make the envelope visible again, right before CRISTINA's eyes. HE watches her calmly sew on the button.)

CRISTINA: Is it one o'clock yet?

BERNARD: Ten till...

(Looking at his watch)

CRISTINA: Fine. I have time.

(There's a silence. BERNARD looks at CRISTINA a bit perplexed. CRISTINA, without looking up from what she's doing, seems to be laughing to herself.)

BERNARD: What's so funny?

CRISTINA *(Laughing)*: Oh, nothing. You should hear what Enrique says...

(SHE stops. BERNARD waits impatiently for the end of the sentence.)

BERNARD: What does he say?
CRISTINA: It's silly. You wouldn't understand anyhow...

(SHE laughs again softly. There's another silence much more tense this time ISABEL has looked up from her book. SHE exchanges a look with BERNARD, who is furious. ISABEL just smiles.)

BERNARD: And *you*. What do you find so amusing? Something else I wouldn't understand?
ISABEL: Perhaps it's the same thing.

(BERNARD is about to explode. The entrance of GERVASIO from right forestalls it. GERVASIO is carrying the silver tray with the day's mail, as in the first act. HE places the tray on the table and starts to leave.)

AURELIA: Gervasio!
GERVASIO: Madam?...
AURELIA: Why don't you do something about lunch? It's almost one o'clock.
GERVASIO: Very well, Madam.
PEDRO *(Laying the newspaper on his knees)*: We can have a late lunch today..
AURELIA: Why?
PEDRO: I don't have much appetite. When nothing's going on, eating can be an excellent solution to boredom...like on an ocean liner. But right now I'm interested in seeing how it all turns out...
AURELIA *(Quickly pointing to the newspaper)*: The crisis in the Middle East?..
PEDRO: Yes. Of course. The Middle East crisis.
AURELIA: Nothing's going to happen. You'll see.
PEDRO: I intend to see. *(To GERVASIO.)* We'll have lunch at the same time as the Egyptians.
GERVASIO *(Not understanding)*: What time is that?
PEDRO: Don't be a fool, Gervasio. Ask in the kitchen. They'll surely know there
AURELIA: Of course they will. They know why they're paid.
GERVASIO *(Who hasn't understood a single word, but manages not to show it very much.)*: Of course, Madam.

(HE exits right.)

BERNARD *(To CRISTINA)*: The mail has arrived...
CRISTINA: So I see... *(BERNARD picks up the tray and offers it to CRISTINA SHE looks at him without making the slightest move to take it.)* What am I supposed to do?

BERNARD: Don't you want to check it?

CRISTINA (*With marked indifference*): No. Why should I? (*BERNARD nervous, withdraws the tray. CRISTINA, quickly.*) Wait! Let me see! (*Encouraged, BERNARD offers her the tray again. CRISTINA doesn't touch the letters. SHE only points to the one on top.*) What an unusual stamp! From Cuba. It's red and has a cigar...

BERNARD (*Trying too hard*): I can't imagine who it's from. Maybe a woman...

CRISTINA: With a cigar on the stamp? I doubt it. It's probably from a man. A business man. Let me have it. (*SHE takes the envelope and tears off the stamp. BERNARD is left holding the tray. Reading the stamp in a loud voice.*) Republic of Cuba...five centavos.

BERNARD (*Extending the tray*): What about the others? Aren't you interested?

CRISTINA (*Putting the letter back on the tray*): Not in the slightest.

(*BERNARD, now in a bad mood, puts the tray back on the table with a thud. CRISTINA has left the stamp on the table. DOÑA AURELIA hands DON PEDRO his stamp album.*)

AURELIA: Some where I heard that Cuba has issued a new five-cent stamp...Do you have one?

PEDRO (*Without taking the album*): I don't think so. Don't bother me now...

AURELIA (*Returning the album to its place*): I can see this isn't one of your philatelic days...

PEDRO: No. Today I'm mad about Natural History.

CRISTINA (*Finishing with the button*): There! Here you are!

(*SHE hands the coat to BERNARD. When HE takes it, HE manages to let the letter fall out of the pocket, close to CRISTINA.*)

BERNARD: Thanks.

CRISTINA: Don't mention it. Oh, you dropped something. (*SHE picks up the letter and hands it to BERNARD as HE is putting on his jacket. HE looks at CRISTINA without taking the letter.*) Here! (*BERNARD unable to control his fury, takes the envelope and stuffs it in his pocket.*) And be careful. It keeps falling out. If it's an important business letter... (*SHE smells her fingers.*) God! How awful! What a revolting perfume! (*SHE puts away her sewing equipment and stands up.*) Well, I'll see you later...

BERNARD: Where're you going?

CRISTINA: For a walk.

BERNARD: Can I go with you?

CRISTINA: Why? I'm only going down to the rose arbor. Goodbye, Isabel.

ISABEL (*Reading, indifferent*): Goodbye.

CRISTINA *(Smells her hand again)*: You've stopped using "Bon Soir, Amour," haven't you?
ISABEL: Yes.
CRISTINA: What's it called?
ISABEL: "A Kiss in The Dark."
CRISTINA.: Very penetrating. *(To BERNARD)* "A Kiss in The Dark." It smells just like the cologne you were using last night.
BERNARD *(trying to make a joke of it)*: I wanted to surprise you with something new...
CRISTINA *(From the door)*: I don't advise that. The danger with surprises is that one never knows who is going to end up most surprised.

(SHE exits gaily. BERNARD watches her speechless. HE turns to ISABEL. SHE pretends to be absorbed in her book.)

BERNARD: Did you hear that, Isabel?
ISABEL *(Indifferent)*: Yes. It sounds to me like Enrique.
BERNARD: I'm talking about the rose arbor.
ISABEL: So?...
BERNARD *(Nervous)*: Our rose arbor.
ISABEL: Ours? I don't understand you.

(SHE goes back to her reading. BERNARD thinks HE's figuring it out and looks over at DOÑA AURELIA and DON PEDRO.)

BERNARD: Aha!

(DOÑA AURELIA and DON PEDRO have been hanging on every word; and when BERNARD catches them watching, THEY quickly try to pretend indifference. DOÑA AURELIA resumes her embroidery. DON PEDRO coughs--a very forced cough this time--while he picks up his paper and hides behind it. BERNARD paces back and forth nervously, whistling a popular tune badly.)

ISABEL *(Irritated, without losing her coldness)*: Bernard!
BERNARD *(Stopping)*: Yes?
ISABEL: Can't you whistle more softly...or better? At least warn me when you're going to whistle, so that I'll be prepared.
BERNARD *(Offended)*: Next you'll be telling me I don't have an ear for music..
ISABEL: Your ear may be all right, but the rest is a disaster.

(BERNARD is once more on the verge of an outburst. ISABEL pretends to read again.)

AURELIA *(To DON PEDRO)*: I was thinking that a little sun might do you good...
PEDRO: Do you think so?
AURELIA: Oh, yes. There's not much you can do here at the moment.
PEDRO: You're probably right. But just a quick stroll, eh?

(THEY get up and go out on the terrace. DON PEDRO turns in the direction CRISTINA took.)

AURELIA: Not to the rose arbor, Pedro. That wouldn't be proper at this hour.
PEDRO: Proper?
AURELIA: I meant healthy...

(THEY go in the opposite direction. ISABEL and BERNARD wait until they are out of sight. ISABEL looks up from her book)

ISABEL: Well, let's have it. What are you thinking?
BERNARD: Didn't you hear? They're together.

(ISABEL smiles at the irony)

ISABEL: ...in our rose arbor. What are you afraid of? That they'll give a repeat performance of our script? Do you think we have a monopoly on illicit kisses? *(BERNARD starts for the garden doors.)* Where are you going, Bernard? *(HE stops and turns around to face her.)* Is it possible that you're so dumb, or blind, that it hasn't occurred to you that they may not be together in the rose arbor?
BERNARD: Then where are they?
ISABEL: They may not be together at all...and, if they are, it may mean nothing at all... *(BERNARD looks at her questioningly.)* Because there's nothing between them. Don't you see? It's only a new game Cristina invented when she caught on to us...to what she thinks is our game...
BERNARD *(With an involuntary expression of revived hope)*: Is it possible?
ISABEL: Didn't you realize when she ignored the letter that she wasn't concerned with her own jealousy anymore but with yours? *(BERNARD, happy, has the impulse to go toward the garden. ISABEL, with resentment)* Run after her. Find her...Ask her forgiveness. *(BERNARD hesitates, a bit ashamed, and turns toward ISABEL.)* Ask her forgiveness for the only thing you can-- without confessing: for the joke you've played on her. Find her and hold her in your arms. And have the courage to kiss her in front of me as you did last night...
BERNARD *(Confused)*: She was going up to bed...
ISABEL: She was going up to wait for you...awake.

BERNARD (*Not knowing what to say*): What's bothering you, Isabel?

ISABEL: What do you think's bothering me? That the slightest spark of jealousy, lighted in the most vulgar way imaginable, has been enough to put you in such a state that you can't even pretend you aren't mad about her...or stupid about her.

BERNARD (*Finding a justification*): She *is* my wife.

ISABEL: Wasn't she your wife the day you took a fancy to me?

BERNARD: Isabel...

ISABEL: Or did your masculine vanity drive you to it? Or maybe you thought it was love when you held me in your arms. But she was your wife then as much as she is now. And you managed to forget it. But I didn't. Because I knew I'd eventually be shortchanged. I counted all the risks. I thought of all the ways it could end: from boredom, indifference, a burst of anger, losing you to another woman. All except one.

BERNARD: Which one?

ISABEL: That you would fall in love with your wife again. I could be resigned to it if another woman took you away from me...but your own wife! It makes me look like a fool! The world is full of women you could have deceived me with--anyone--except her. You've sacrificed me to her.

(*SHE takes out a handkerchief and puts it to her eyes.*)

BERNARD (*uncomfortable*): Tears, Isabel?

ISABEL (*Angry at herself*): Can't you see? Yes, I'm crying, so that none of the details are missing. I've given up my last defenses. I have no dignity left...Tears are stupid and worthless...They only get on a man's nerves and destroy the last hope. Then a door slams and a man stands behind it, with a deep sigh of relief--liberated.

BERNARD (*Going close to her*): Isabel...

ISABEL (*Drying her eyes and recovering her strength*): Leave me alone! What more do you want? Now that you can't give me love, you'll try compassion...and feel strong and proud of yourself. Or maybe you'll cut a notch in the wall like a fighter pilot after he's shot down another enemy plane. (*BERNARD is worried.*) What are you thinking about?

BERNARD: I'm sorry...

ISABEL: For her?

BERNARD (*Who no longer sees the need to pretend*): Do you think she was the one we heard in the rose arbor last night?

ISABEL: Yes.

BERNARD: And thus she still believes it was all a game?

ISABEL: Was your kiss part of the game, Bernard?

BERNARD (*Flatly*): No.

ISABEL: She knows your kisses better than anyone. Do you suppose she was fooled? *(BERNARD doesn't answer. ISABEL concentrates her vengeance into a single idea, and measures her words, one by one.)* That kiss is what I'll leave between you and her.
BERNARD: She'll never be sure...
ISABEL *(With a hard smile)*: And you think that won't matter?

(BERNARD is left silent and defenseless. DOÑA AURELIA and DON PEDRO enter upstage. ISABEL dries her eyes hastily and starts speaking in a light, superficial manner. The OLDER COUPLE return to their habitual places and occupations. ISABEL, almost laughing, as if she'd just finished telling a very amusing story.)

ISABEL: And the poor idiot thought he could go right back to his wife as if nothing had happened... *(ENRIQUE enters right in time to hear almost all that ISABEL has been saying.)* But he hadn't counted on a retaliatory strike from her...She'd made up her mind that very day...
ENRIQUE: Do I know this story?
ISABEL: I'm not sure.
ENRIQUE: I don't like risque stories...especially when I've heard them before, *(HE starts toward the garden.)*
ISABEL: Where are you going?
ENRIQUE: Outside...to see what Cristina wants...
ISABEL: Don't bother.
ENRIQUE: Ah...no?
ISABEL: No.
ENRIQUE: So you two have already found out? Did Cristina tell you?
ISABEL: No.
ENRIQUE *(To ISABEL)*: You guessed it...of course! *(HE goes over and kisses her.)* You're a genius! What a pity you're my wife. How nice it would be to fall in love with you! *(HE takes out his notebook and jots down the line. To BERNARD.)* So you really fell for it?
BERNARD *(Vexed)*: Why not?
ENRIQUE: You're in love with Cristina, and when we're in love our minds can't deal with practical matters. *(To ISABEL.)* That's why I had to give up thinking about you. We would have died of starvation. *(To BERNARD.)* Well, now that you know that it was all a joke, why don't you go look for her, and provide us with a tender scene of reconciliation. Isabel will love it. She has a special fondness for happy endings. *(To ISABEL.)* Don't you dear?
ISABEL *(Pointedly)*: Yes. It'll be charming...for a while.
ENRIQUE: Naturally. We have no interest in other people's love, since it usually ends up as a bad imitation of our own. *(BERNARD, on the verge of*

committing violence, exits upstage without saying a word to anybody. ENRIQUE not understanding his reaction.) What's wrong with him now?

ISABEL: He's afraid that Cristina knows that he's really been unfaithful to her.

ENRIQUE *(Without showing much surprise)*: Really! I thought as much!...When did it happen?

ISABEL: Last winter.

ENRIQUE: And who was the woman? Do you know?

ISABEL: No.

ENRIQUE: Not even a suspicion?

ISABEL: It's a big city...But I think it was with the wife of a friend of his.

ENRIQUE: Of course! It's what always happens to men who're too faithful to their wives. Since they're together constantly, there are so few opportunities...so it really has to be a friend of the family... *(HE embraces ISABEL.)* You'll never find the women I've deceived you with. It's the least I can do for you...and for them.

ISABEL *(Slipping quickly from his arms)*: We should leave here.

ENRIQUE: If you wish.

ISABEL: Today.

ENRIQUE: So soon? Why?

ISABEL: Don't you understand? When the truth comes out, things may turn violent...

ENRIQUE: Why should the truth come out? Of course, he's so inexperienced...

ISABEL: He's afraid someone will tell her...some spiteful friend...or the woman herself.

ENRIQUE: Well, we can't let on that we know. What excuse can we use for leaving so suddenly?

ISABEL: Didn't you bring along the telegram we always use when we get bored with a place and want to leave?

ENRIQUE: Of course. I keep it in my suitcase, for emergencies. But it's beginning to look terribly used. No one's going to believe a boy just brought it from the telegraph office...unless he dragged it all the way on the ground. Besides, it says: Lola critical. Operation tomorrow. Uncle Tony.

ISABEL: What's wrong with that?

ENRIQUE: They know very well that Aunt Lola recovered from her operation.

ISABEL: Maybe she's had a relapse.

ENRIQUE: They also know that Uncle Tony died last year. So it would be particularly odd to have a message from him.

ISABEL: Oh, I don't know. Where he is they probably get the news in advance.

ENRIQUE: You do want them to know that we've made up an excuse, don't you?...

ISABEL: Yes, but in their frame of mind they won't question anything we do.

ENRIQUE: You're expecting the worst...

ISABEL: Oh, yes!

ENRIQUE: Poor dears! Listen, do you suppose there's anything we could do to help?...

ISABEL: It would be difficult. It depends on whether I could talk with her before they meet.

ENRIQUE: Well, try. If only you could! The poor girl's going to be terribly upset. I'm not concerned about how he feels. These amateurs, with lack of experience, are the ones who ruin the theatre for the professionals. I wouldn't be surprised if you started distrusting me. That's the effect bad examples have.

ISABEL: I promise you I won't. Get our bags packed and have them put in the car...and don't forget the telegram.

ENRIQUE: Couldn't we say we had a long distance call?

ISABEL: Where do you expect to find a telephone?

ENRIQUE: True. But it's a more modern kind of lie. *(HE looks toward the garden.)* I'll leave you with her. Do what you can.

ISABEL: I intend to do everything I can.

(ENRIQUE exits right. ISABEL goes toward the garden in search of CRISTINA.)

PEDRO: Have you ever watched a spider stalk a fly? It's fascinating.

AURELIA: No. It's painful. I feel sorry for the fly...

PEDRO: And weren't you wishing that winter would come so that you'd be free of them?

AURELIA: It's just that I can't put up with spider's web...the trickery, the lies...

PEDRO: And what if the spider catches her victim with the truth?

AURELIA: That's worse. Truth is a dangerous weapon which shouldn't be permitted in just anyone's hands. The more important the truth, the more care one should take with it. All truths should be collected and put in the hands of specialists.

PEDRO: What about the rest of us?

AURELIA: We'll get along nicely with our little white lies. And when we get tired of them we can exchange them for others...carefully disinfected, or course.

(SHE stops talking den she hears ISABEL and CRISTINA coming from the garden.)

ISABEL: ...he went out to look for you as soon as he found out. Because he hadn't doubted you for a moment.

CRISTINA: No?

ISABEL: You can feel proud about that...but don't be too sure of yourself. It's bad for them to trust us too much. Thieves are the most trusting people in the world. If they were afraid their own houses would be robbed, they wouldn't go out to steal in the first place.

CRISTINA: I never had doubts about him either.

ISABEL: You should have. Husbands with a fidelity complex, like yours, are the most prone to deceiving their wives...and the other woman. They're always leaving and coming back.

CRISTINA: They do come back!

ISABEL: The ones who don't come back are really the faithful ones. Leaving for good is a form of fidelity...at least to infidelity. It's better than all those small deceptions that we end up getting used to.

CRISTINA: Is it possible to get used to that?

ISABEL: You can get used to anything. The first infidelity is the one that truly hurts--like seeing the first scratch on an expensive piece of luggage. Then we realize there's nothing to be done about it, that the luggage is destined to be covered with the stickers of all the hotels where he's spent the night.

CRISTINA: But until that first infidelity actually happens...

ISABEL: Do we really know when it happens? Or, if we think we know, can we be sure it's the first time? Men are masters at that game. The moment they're out of sight, anything can happen.

CRISTINA: And if they're right beside us?

ISABEL: Well, it might have happened under our very nose. Men never deny themselves an adventure if there's no inconvenience involved. That's why we have to beware of the house across the street, the apartment next door-- our closest friend.

CRISTINA: You're my closest friend.

ISABEL: Well, you shouldn't trust me, because I can't help being a woman. Being on guard may not keep you from getting hurt, but you won't be caught by surprise...

CRISTINA: There's a better way, Isabel.

ISABEL: And what is it?

CRISTINA: Trusting. Believing because you want to believe. Can you understand that?

ISABEL: Men are good at making us believe what we want to believe, even when they are lying.

CRISTINA: Some men, perhaps. But he's not like the rest.

ISABEL: Then if your best friend told you...

CRISTINA: She'd be lying. And she'd have her own reasons for lying.

ISABEL: The same reasons she'd have for telling the truth.

CRISTINA: Her words would be tainted by those reasons. They'd be meaningless.

ISABEL: Very pretty, Cristina. But not very practical. That's nothing more than blind faith.

CRISTINA: They always picture Faith that way, with a blindfold over her eyes.

ISABEL: Like Love.

CRISTINA: But Love is only a child. Faith is a woman.

ISABEL: Love carries a bow and arrows. Faith is unarmed.

CRISTINA: There's no need, She's never going to fight. Don't you see that she's the stronger one?

ISABEL: Stronger than Love?

CRISTINA: Stronger than what some women call Love.

(There is a short silence. A silence that ISABEL has calculated before she responds.)

ISABEL: Do you know that I'm leaving?

CRISTINA: When?

ISABEL: Today. In a little while.

CRISTINA: I'm sorry...

ISABEL: Are you really sorry?

CRISTINA: Why would I be glad? I know you're not taking anything with you.

ISABEL: I may be leaving something behind...

CRISTINA: It's possible. Well, if I find it, I'll send it on to you right away. If it's yours, it wouldn't be of any use to me. Our measurements are quite different.

(Without replying, ISABEL has gone toward the doorway at right. Near the doorway, SHE turns around slowly and looks at CRISTINA. SHE lets her words drop with a smiling sweetness.)

ISABEL: Ah, I forgot to tell you. Yesterday, at sundown, when you came close to the rose arbor, we heard you coming...

CRISTINA *(With happiness)*: You did? *(Almost touched)* Thank you, Isabel. *(ISABEL doesn't move, as if she still had something to say. CHRISTINE understands it, and her happiness turns to doubt.)* Before...or after?

ISABEL *(Smiling maliciously)*: After.

(SHE exits right, after having savored the effect of her words on CRISTINA. CRISTINA, under the weight of ISABEL's revelation, bows her head. DOÑA AURELIA and DON PEDRO are also crushed. BERNARD enters rapidly from the garden. When HE sees CRISTINA, HE stops.)

BERNARD *(From the door, showing his happiness)*: Cristina!

(SHE looks up and turns to BERNARD with such an expression that HE understands at once. THEY stand there looking at each other without daring to speak. After this brief and tense silence, DON PEDRO turns to DOÑA AURELIA.)

PEDRO: When I returned...
AURELIA: Yes?
PEDRO: I understood, when I saw you, that you knew everything...
AURELIA: Except the gory details.
PEDRO: I came with my heart in hand.
AURELIA: Because you'd gotten it back and didn't know what to do with it.

(CRISTINA and BERNARD fully realize the intent of the words of DON
PEDRO and DOÑA AURELIA. THEY listen with growing interest and, at
certain moments, react with the words as if THEY were speaking them.)

PEDRO: I felt as if I had just been born.
AURELIA: For me it was more like dying...I was waiting for a word from you.
PEDRO: And I couldn't say a thing.
AURELIA.: Because it would have hurt you too much.
PEDRO: Less than it would have hurt you to hear it.
AURELIA: You didn't even ask me to forgive you.
PEDRO: Did I need to?
AURELIA: No. But you could have helped a little.
PEDRO: You did forgive me.
AURELIA: Yes, without having a good reason.
PEDRO: You did the right thing.
AURELIA: The problem was I had to do the right thing several times before it
    was over.
PEDRO.: You kept your wonderful dignity through it all.
AURELIA: Dignity costs more than you know. Did you understand why I forgave
    you?
PEDRO: Because you loved me.
AURELIA (Shaking her head): Wrong. At that moment I hated you as much as
    I'd ever loved you. I had to put something on the scale to find my
    equilibrium. But it was better to take you back, loving you less, than to part
    while I loved you still. It's dangerous to play everything on a single
    moment, on one card. A deck has forty. More or less the number of years
    two people can be together. I forgave you because I looked ahead, and I saw
    the difference that remained to walk together, one supporting the other, so
    that we wouldn't fall...or if we fell to get up and go.
PEDRO: You thought of all that in such a short time?
AURELIA: No. It was simple. I thought of my parents. I remembered them
    happy, inseparable, at a point in life when they were immune to the hurts
    from the outside. I pictured you old, for a moment.
PEDRO: Sure, old and stuffed like a hunting trophy.
AURELIA: I also pictured myself old at your side. And how happy I was to still
    be young and to have the strength to go the rest of the way!

PEDRO: And then you put your arms around me.

AURELIA (*Protesting*): *You* did that, Pedro.

PEDRO (*Also protesting*): I beg your pardon, it was...

AURELIA: It's true. We both did. One look was enough. It was as if we were standing on springs.

(*CRISTINA and BERNARD look at each other. As if moved by an electrical shock.*)

(*THEY fall into each other's arms passionately. THEY remain that way, united, calmly, until the end of the play. DOÑA AURELIA and DON PEDRO look at each other and smile. ENRIQUE appears in the doorway at right with his raincoat over arm and cap in hand. After a moment of surprise, HE breaks into a smile and summons ISABEL with a gesture of his hand. SHE appears in the doorway. SHE is dressed in her travelling clothes and is carrying a large bag in her hand. ENRIQUE points to the embracing COUPLE. ISABEL can't hide her anger. SHE crosses brusquely and exits upstage without turning her head. ENRIQUE, a little puzzled, follows her but stops in the doorway. DOÑA AURELIA and DON PEDRO stand up. GERVASIO returns through the garden entrance and is about to go out again at right.*)

PEDRO (*To GERVASIO*): Gervasio... (*GERVASIO stops.*) Set the dining room table for four. And bring up a bottle of that good champagne...the kind I said we didn't have.

GERVASIO (*Indicating with a gesture that the weekend guests are departing.*): But sir. If...If you and Madam are alone!...

AURELIA: It's because we're alone, Gervasio. That's what we're celebrating...being alone...together.

(*GERVASIO, without understanding, bows and exits right. DON PEDRO and DOÑA AURELIA embrace too. ENRIQUE watches them with obvious delight. From offstage an impatient car horn. ENRIQUE looks toward the garden, but then looks back. HE observes the two embracing couples. HE looks at his wrist watch and with his right hand, index finger extended, HE begins to count like a boxing referee. Offstage, frenetic and deafening, a car horn.*)

CURTAIN

CRITICAL REACTION IN SPAIN AND THE UNITED STATES

"(López Rubio) has achieved with the play that opened last night...not only hi best work for the stage, but also one of the tersest, most intelligent...theatrica works of our time. *Celos del aire* has a perfect and legitimate right to join the ranks of the best theatre, without ceding in merit to any foreign play of the same scope and type."

> Alfredo Marquerie
> *ABC* (Madrid)
> 26 January 1950

"It is a wonder something so clever took so long to cross the Atlantic. The stor is about the games people play. Games in this case which are inspired b boredom, underlined by truth and punctuated by love...Nothing, including laughte appears to have been lost in this translation of 'Pyrenees.'"

> Mark Bonne
> Northwest Herald (Illinois)
> 12 August 1986

"All that happens in this comedy by a master, José López Rubio, gives off an a of freshness, of sincerity...The mastery in the dialogue, witty, unabashedly soulfu serves with precision the development of the four young characters who, in certain manner, repeat without realizing it, the old game of infidelity, jealousy an reconciliation of Doña Aurelia and Don Pedro, the 'invisible' couple in who house they are spending their brief vacation...Time has not passed for this play spite of the profound process of moral change experienced by society in rece years."

> Lorenzo López Sancho
> *ABC* (Madrid)
> 28 December 1990

ABOUT THE TRANSLATOR

Marion Peter Holt is a member of the doctoral faculty in Theatre at the Graduate Center of the City University of New York and professor of Spanish Literature and Translation at CUNY's College of Staten Island. He has also taught "Translation for the Stage" in the Interdisciplinary Program in Translation at the Graduate Center. In 1985, *Choice* named his collection *Antonio Buero-Valleio: Three Plays* an outstanding university press book of the year. His translations of contemporary Spanish and Latin American plays have been staged in New York and London and by major regional theatres in the United States. In 1986 he was elected a corresponding member of the Real Academia Española.

TRANSLATOR'S NOTE

This translation of *Celos del aire* was originally undertaken at the request of the Writers Theatre, an energetic group of young professionals based in New York. This company sponsored a staged reading with an outstanding cast, providing an opportunity to test the playability of the dialogue; a second staged reading was presented by Seattle's Intiman Theatre Company as part of its "New Plays Onstage" series. In August 1988, *In August We Play the Pyrenees* opened for a four-week run at the Shady Lane Playhouse (Marengo, Illinois).

Although López Rubio's comedy is set in a remote area of Spain, the tone of the play is international, and only minor adjustments have been necessary for English-speaking audiences. In the feigned love scene that ends Act II, the incorrigible self-dramatizer Enrique recites to the cooperative Cristina the names of the provinces of Spain--not all of which would be recognizable to audiences outside Spain. For the English version I have substituted the capitals of Europe, while adding a slight twist in the final line. (Directors may want to make a few adjustments in light of recent developments in Germany and the Soviet Union.) The confrontation scene between Cristina and Isabel in Act III has been slightly abbreviated.

While the original title has a special resonance for Spanish audiences, its literal translation does not have any particular suggestions for theatergoers in the United States or Britain. The new title provides its own hints, completely in keeping with the spirit of this unabashedly metatheatrical play. The actual playing time for this brisk but subtle comedy in the present version, not counting one or two intermissions or intervals, is no more than two hours.

M.P.H.

ACKNOWLEDGEMENTS

I wish to express my appreciation to Martha T. Halsey for the efforts that have made possible the initiation of the *Estreno* Translation Series; To Phyllis Zatlin for her introduction to *In August We Play the Pyrenees*; and to Robert E. Dixon of Penn State's Center for Computing Assistance in Liberal Arts for his expert work in reformatting the original manuscript of the play for publication, while keeping it entirely suitable for use as an acting script.

M. P. H.

ESTRENO:
CUADERNOS DEL TEATRO
ESPAÑOL CONTEMPORANEO

Published at Penn State University
Martha Halsey, Ed.
Phyllis Zatlin, Assoc. Ed.

A journal featuring play texts of previously unpublished works from contemporary Spain, interviews withplaywrights, directors, and critics, and extensive critical studies in both Spanish and English.

Plays published have included texts by Buero-Vallejo, Sastre, Arrabal, Gala, Nieva, Salom, Martín Recuerda, Olmo, Martínez Mediero, F. Cabal, P. Pedrero and Onetti. The journal carries numerous photographs of recent play performances in Spain and elsewhere, including performances in translation.

Also featured are an annual bibliography, regular book reviews, and critiques of the recent theater season, as well as a round table in which readers from both the U. S. and Spain share information and engage in lively debates.

ESTRENO also publishes a series of translations of contemporary Spanish plays which may be subscribed to separately.

Please mail to: ESTRENO
                   350 N. Burrowes Bldg.
                   University Park, PA 16802
                   USA.

Individual subscriptions are $14.00 and institutional subscriptions, $26.00 for the calendar year.

Name   _____

Address   _____

            _____

<u>ESTRENO</u>: CONTEMPORARY SPANISH PLAYS SERIES

General Editor: Martha Halsey

No. 1   Jaime Salom: BONFIRE AT DAWN
          Translated by Phyllis Zatlin

No. 2   José López Rubio: IN AUGUST WE PLAY THE
          PYRENEES
          Translated by Marion P. Holt

No. 3   Ramón del Valle-Inclán: SAVAGE ACTS: FOUR
          ONE-ACT PLAYS
          Translated by Robert Lima

    A continuing series representing Spanish plays of
several generations and varying theatrical approaches
selected for their potential interest to American audiences.
Published every 9-12 months.
    Forthcoming plays will include works of Buero-Vallejo,
Antonio Gala, Paloma Pedrero and others.

    Subscriptions: Standing orders for the series or orders
for individual plays should be sent to:

<u>ESTRENO</u>
350 N. Burrowes Bldg.
University Park, PA 16802
U. S. A.

$6.00 per play including postage.

PLAYS OF THE NEW DEMOCRATIC SPAIN (1975-1990)

Contents

Editor's Prologue   Patricia W. O'Connor
Introduction   Felicia Londré

Hardback .... 57.58 (+ tax)
Paperback .... 32.50 (+ tax)*
* Special discount for Estreno readers:
Paperback 28.00

Orders:

Estreno
Department of Romance Languages (ML 377)
University of Cincinnati
Cincinnati, OH 45221
U. S. A.